A Theology of Christian Prayer

A Theology
of Christian Prayer

John H. Wright, S.J.

Pueblo Publishing Company

New York

Design: Frank Kacmarcik

For the memory of my parents
May and Ivan Wright

Contents

Introduction

Few areas of theology are as crucial and critical as that of
prayer. We here touch our central relationship with
God. What you think about prayer necessarily involves
what you think about God and your relationship to
him.* It already says very much about how you conceive of God if you think that prayer to him is significantly important, if you think it really makes any
difference. For you are saying that God in some sense
hears us, is personally concerned about us, answers
us, is at work in the world in response to us. You are
saying in fact that prayer is life with the living God.
This, of course, is what the Bible teaches about God
and prayer. But how can we as men and women of
the last quarter of the twentieth century understand
and appropriate this teaching? This is the central
question of this book. The main concern here is understanding rather than technique; it is a "what"
book, rather than a "how to" book. No doubt, many
"how to's" follow from this "what," but they are not
the main area of investigation.

Our contemporary culture looks upon prayer as a very
questionable form of activity. We are beset by a prevail-
ing secularism, an attitude of mind that puts God at a
distance, removes him from what goes on in the world,
separates him from human society and human history.
If God is not dead, he appears to be absent. And in this
atmosphere, prayer easily withers and dies. There is no
way to relate to an absent God or to live with him. If
prayer continues at all in this situation it easily becomes
either a matter of autosuggestion, or a cry in the dark,
uttered simply because it is too painful to remain silent.

*The use of masculine pronouns for God is retained in this
book for smoothness and consistency. It is not a theological
statement, but a limitation of the English language at its
present stage of development.

If it becomes autosuggestion we go through the forms of prayer because it makes us feel good, gives us a sense of safety and assurance, induces an attitude of confidence that makes living possible, even if in our heart of hearts we feel that the whole thing is fantasy. If it continues only as a cry in the dark, then loneliness, helplessness, the absurdity and injustice of life make us call out, like persons lost in the night, in the hope that someone may hear us and answer us. It is not the cry of faith, but the cry of despair.

Secularism has many roots. Many of these are good in themselves, raise valid and important questions, and hence need to be incorporated somehow into our world view. If we failed to do this we would become aliens to our own age, vainly trying to live in another century and another world of thought. Chief among these roots of secularism are science and technology. Albert Einstein wrote:

"The main source of the present-day conflicts between the spheres of religion and of science lies in this concept of a personal God. It is the aim of science to establish general rules which determine the reciprocal connections of objects and events in time and space . . .

"The more a man is imbued with the ordered regularity of all events, the firmer becomes his conviction that there is no room left by the side of this ordered regularity for causes of a different nature. For him neither the rule of human nor the rule of divine will exist as an independent cause of natural events. To be sure, the doctrine of a personal God interfering with natural events could never be *refuted*, in the real sense, by science, for this doctrine can always take refuge in those domains in which scientific knowledge has not yet been able to set foot."[1]

"There is no room left," he tells us, for God to exist and act in the universe. What can prayer then possiby mean

xiv

to a person of scientific outlook? But to reject this outlook means trying to live at some other time, in some other age and culture.

Technology, an outgrowth of modern science, tends to induce an attitude of mastery and self-sufficiency that is not easily compatible with prayer. Through a developing control over the processes of nature, through incredible achievements in communication, transportation, manufacturing, medicine, building, and so on, technology makes us feel that we can get through our own efforts whatever we have need of, that we are not indebted to or dependent upon any source for our well-being. Prayer of whatever sort seems strangely inappropriate in this setting. We don't feel inclined to thank God for anything we have or to ask him for anything we need. We have gotten what we worked for; we must rely on our own efforts and ingenuity for what more we desire. Prayer is for those who can do nothing else.

Two other roots of modern secularism may be mentioned: the dimensions of the problem of evil in the world today, and an inherited view of God as eternal and unchangeable. The nineteenth century seemed gripped by a myth of endless progress and development. The theory of evolution and the study of history reinforced an idea of indefinite and irreversible upward growth. This fitted in neatly with a providence guiding all things surely to a golden age in the near future. But global war, economic oppression, racial hatred and discrimination, exploitation and pollution of the environment, hunger, corruption in high places, have exploded the myth of inevitable progress and given new force to the problem of evil: if there is an all wise and all good and powerful God, how is this enormous tide of evil possible? We seem very much on our own, with no divine presence and guidance helping us.

Certain philosophical views of God, derived from aspects of Greek thought, have found an unsuspected place in our unconscious or subconscious attitudes. God is said to be infinite, eternal, unchangeable, utterly transcendent. All these things are true, if understood properly. But they easily become translated into "remote, uninvolved, unaffected," which they need not mean at all. But when they are understood in this way they make prayer impossible; for how can I pray to one who is completely isolated in himself, unaffected by anything I might say or do, radically unconcerned about my life and destiny. And if the Scriptures seem to say otherwise, these are explained as metaphors or anthropomorphisms which are suited to our lack of understanding, but are not truly revelatory of the nature of God. This way of viewing God contributes to the secularism of the age, because it removes God from the world in any way that really counts.

The questions raised by these sources of today's secularist mentality are real and deserve real answers. But before we capitulate and abandon the biblical teaching and practice of prayer, we need to consider more carefully what this prayer tradition really says, and then see whether we can respond to the problems raised by science, technology, evil, and divine transcendence. We should not allow some extraneous bias, whether of science or of metaphysics, to determine what our view of prayer must be; we rely for this on the Word of God. But these other considerations can spur us to seek more deeply the meaning of our words, to discover how we can in our age as people of this culture continue to be men and women of prayer.

NOTES

1. Albert Einstein, "Science and Religion, II," in *Out of My Later Years* (New York: Philosophical Library, 1950), pp. 27, 28.

Chapter One

Prayer in the Old Testament: A Study of Cases

To get at the outset a concrete sense of the meaning of prayer in the Bible we will consider some examples of men and women of prayer as described there, and then draw some conclusions from these examples which can serve as background and guidelines for the rest of the book. It would be easy enough to sustain the thesis that all the great men and women of the Bible were persons of prayer. In the great majority of cases, this is explicitly shown; in others it is clearly implied. But since to consid er all cases would be extremely long, we select some of the more important of these people as case studies in prayer. From the Old Testament we will consider the founding patriarch, Abraham; the great liberator of the people, Moses; his sister and helper, Miriam; Hannah, the mother of the prophet Samuel; David the king; his son Solomon; Jeremiah, prophet of the last days of Jerusalem; and Judith, heroine of a didactic story of God's protective strength. In the next chapter we will look at just two persons of the New Testament, who sum up in themselves the whole biblical teaching: Jesus and Mary. Various and rich as these cases are, from them emerge basic insights into the meaning of prayer everywhere in the biblical tradition.

SCRIPTURE AND THEOLOGY
Since there are a number of different approaches to the use of Scripture in the work of theology it seems valu- able to indicate from the beginning which approach we will be using throughout this book. One approach endeavors through the use of historical-critical tools to

discover exactly what happened in the events narrated in the Bible. What actually took place when the Hebrew people left Egypt? What was the drying up of the Red (or Reed) Sea? What did Moses actually say to Pharaoh? This is a valuable and difficult undertaking that serves to underline the fact that the Hebrew and Christian faiths are rooted in historical happenings. They are not "nature religions" somehow deducible from universal human experience. They grow out of and refer back to once-for-all, not-repeatable human events. This, however, will not be the primary focus in our approach to Scripture.

Another approach, the one we will be consistently employing, aims rather at discovering the faith stance and religious intention of the writers of Scripture, and of those who read them as divinely inspired works. This approach views Scripture primarily as the expression of the faith of the historical community, a community formed and guided by the Holy Spirit. Faith stance concerns primarily the *meaning* of events, not their detailed and exact description. Evidently, for biblical faith some kernel of actual event is necessary, for it is impossible to talk about the meaning of an event if nothing happened at all. If there never was an exodus from Egypt, we cannot talk about it as God's great saving act. But for this it is not necessary to have all the exact details. In fact, biblical writers add details, embellish their story, so as to make the meaning of the event clear. Furthermore, some events assume their full meaning only in the light of subsequent history, and hence the faith version of them will describe them from a perspective not available even to those who were the actual eyewitnesses. This way of recalling and telling stories about things that have happened is the ordinary human way of doing it, even when the things are very important.

Thus, as we consider these figures of the Old and New Testaments, we need not suppose that events happened exactly as they are described. But the description provides us with the meaning of the relationship between God and the events of human history. Sometimes, as in the story of Judith, the particular events never happened at all; we are dealing with a piece of religious, historical fiction. But it contains a vision of divine grace and influence upon history that is drawn by faith from the sweep of Old Testament history and then embedded in this story for the purpose of concise, clear, and vivid instruction. We see what the author was indeed trying to convey: his faith in the meaning of God's presence and action in history, and, for our particular purposes, his faith in the human ability to relate to God in prayer. This is of inestimable value in discovering the meaning and promise of our own lives.

TYPES OF OLD TESTAMENT PRAYER
The Call of Abraham
The call of Abraham, recounted in Genesis 12.1, began the special election of the Hebrew race, descended from him through his son Isaac. God promised Abraham that he would be a blessing and, "By you all the families of the earth shall bless themselves" (Gen. 12.2-3). It was Abraham's vocation somehow to bring blessings upon the other peoples of the earth. Genesis 18.16-33 tells the story of Abraham's prayer for the cities of Sodom and Gomorrah, a prayer he made in response to this vocation. In the biblical account, God makes express reference to this part of his promise as he discloses to Abraham his plan to punish these cities for their sinfulness (cf. Gen. 18.17-21). Abraham appeals to the justice of God as Judge of all the earth not to destroy the innocent with the wicked. He begins with the possibility that fifty righteous men may be found in the cities; will God for their sake spare them all? God's answer was yes. Abraham then proceeded to reduce the number of innocent from fifty to forty-five, to forty, to thirty, to twenty, and finally to ten. In each case God agreed not to de-

stroy the cities for the sake of the innocent few. At this point the Lord went his way, and Abraham returned home (cf. Gen. 18.22-33). In the end not even ten were found, and God destroyed the two cities (Gen. 19.24-28).

What made it possible for Abraham to approach God in prayer was that God had first approached Abraham through the call and promise. Abraham, relying on this, acknowledged the justice and power of God in dealing with human sinfulness and pleaded for mercy. He spoke and bargained with God as if He were another human person, though much greater and more kindly disposed than most of the powerful of that day. From the standpoint of the biblical story, Abraham's prayer failed only because there were not ten just men to be found in the sinful cities.

Moses: A Man of Prayer
Moses is a towering figure in the Old Testament whose influence in the formation of Israel as a united people is incalculable. He is also preeminently a man of prayer. It was said of him later that God talked with him as a man talks with his friend, in the intimacy of face-to-face conversation (cf. Ex. 33.11). The story of his life contains many examples of his prayer, but one of the most noteworthy is in Exodus 32.7-14. Moses had gone up Mount Sinai with Joshua to receive from God the tables of the law (cf. Ex. 24.13). After he had been there some days God revealed to him that in his absence the Israelites, whom He described as "your people, whom you brought up out of the land of Egypt," had made a molten calf and worshiped it (cf. Ex. 32.7-9). God then asks Moses to let Him alone, so that His anger could destroy them and He would make a new great nation from Moses' descendants (Ex. 32.10). In the Scriptures the threats of God are summons to repentance, warnings to be converted and to adopt as one's own God's purpose and attitude; they achieve their purpose when they need not be inflicted. This understanding, coupled with

4

God's unusual request that Moses let Him alone, indicated to Moses that God's real intention was not extermination but purification and conversion. Hence, Moses pleads with God for the Hebrew people, calling them, in clear distinction to the way God had spoken of them, "thy people, whom thou has brought forth out of the land of Egypt with great power and with a mighty hand" (Ex. 32.11). He gives two reasons why God should relent: what the Egyptians would say if God were to destroy the people He brought forth, and more importantly, what God had promised to Abraham, Isaac, and Israel. Moses' prayer turns aside God's anger and He decides not to destroy His people.

This episode makes very clear the power of prayer. God does indeed listen and respond. Even if it does not point to a change of mind in the deeper sense of what God truly wants to accomplish, it shows God responsive to the human condition, truly intending to destroy if renewed prayer and conversion do not remove the cause of his anger. As the rest of the chapter shows, Moses descends from the mountain bearing the purpose of God in his words and deeds. He destroys the idol and eliminates from the people those who persist in their idolatrous frame of mind.

Miriam and Hannah: Praise of God
Two members of Moses' family are close associates in guiding the people through the desert: Aaron, his brother, and Miriam, his sister (cf. Mic. 6.4). It is likely that this is the same sister who had earlier saved the life of the infant Moses when she had spoken with Pharaoh's daughter (cf. Ex. 2.4-8). In Exodus 15.20 she is identified as a prophetess and a sister of Aaron. The occasion is the moment just following the crossing of the Reed Sea and the drowning of the Egyptian troops who had been pursuing the Hebrews. She leads a group of women singing and dancing as an expression of gratitude to God. Biblical criticism judges that the brief song

5

of praise attributed to her on this occasion may well be the composition of an eyewitness:

Sing to the LORD, for he has triumphed gloriously;
The horse and his rider he has thrown into the sea.

(Ex. 15.21)

Her prayer acknowledges the power of God at work in history to protect the Hebrews from their enemies. Implied is the confidence that he will continue to be with them. These implications are drawn in the song attributed to Moses expanding the theme announced by Miriam (cf. Ex. 15.1-18).

One of the most beautiful of Old Testament canticles is placed on the lips of Hannah in 1 Samuel 2.1-10. She is the mother of the prophet Samuel, who will anoint Saul as king, and then many years later anoint David to succeed him. The First Book of Samuel opens by recounting her sadness at being barren. She prayed silently in the shrine at Shiloh that God would give her a son, promising to dedicate him to the Lord's service (cf. 1 Sam. 1.9-11). The priest Eli thought she was drunk because of her distraught state and the soundless movement of her lips. Hannah explained her plight to the priest, and he blessed her, praying that God would grant her petition. This he does to her great joy. Sometime after Samuel's birth, when Hannah has weaned her child, she brings him to the sanctuary at Shiloh to lend him to the Lord as long as he lives. This is the occasion for her great canticle of praise. The central theme is the divine reversal of human values and stations: "The Lord makes poor and makes rich; he brings low, he also exalts. He raises up the poor from the dust; he lifts the needy from the ash heap, to make them sit with princes and inherit a seat of honor" (1 Sam. 2.7-8a). She sees the power of God to dispose of human fortunes rooted in his creative power over the world: "For the pillars of the earth are the Lord's, and on them he has set the world" (v. 8b). God's action in history is a response to the worthiness and

6

unworthiness of his human creatures: "He will guard the feet of his faithful ones; but the wicked shall be cut off in darkness; for not by might shall a man prevail" (v. 9). The actual late composition of this hymn is shown in the final reference to the monarchy: "He will give strength to his king, and exalt the power of his anointed" (v. 10c).

It is said that the greatest claim to fame this canticle has is that it forms the basis of Mary's *Magnificat* in the New Testament. Still it is wonderfully rich in the theology it expresses: God's action in the lives of men and women in response to their actions and in consequence of his universal power as creator and sustainer of the world. It is this fundamental conviction that underlies all theology of prayer as significant human activity in the sight of God.

David: Giving Thanks to God
David is reckoned as the second king of the Israelite nation, succeeding Saul by divine election. It is perhaps more accurate to see Saul as the last of the judges, though he bears the name king, and David as the first real king, who united all twelve tribes and gave them a national capital, the old Jebusite city of Jerusalem. As king he represents in his person the whole nation, for whom he prays as well as for himself. (David as a man given to prayer and the praise of God is a memory celebrated in attributing the entire psalter to his composition. Some psalms may actually date from his time, but their time of writing spans several centuries.) One of the great prayers that Scripture places on the lips of David is his act of thanksgiving after hearing from the prophet Nathan the oracle of promise for his house and his heirs. The unconditioned character of that promise reflected the earlier promise to Abraham, and it served to lighten and encourage the people of Jerusalem for centuries to come. David's prayer of thanksgiving is an interweaving of many themes (cf. 2 Sam. 7.18-29). He thanks God for

all that he has done for him thus far, and especially for the gracious promise concerning the future of his house. He praises God for his great deeds in history, especially in the freeing of Israel from Egypt to make them his people through covenant. He begs that God would continue to bless him, and he intercedes for his house and his nation. It thus sums up in fact the chief kinds of prayer that the Bible contains.

Solomon: Builder of a House of Prayer
Solomon, David's son and successor as king, offered a prayer at the solemn dedication of the temple (cf. 1 Kg. 8.15-53). He recalls much that David expressed in his prayer, but he underlines the great significance of the temple in the prayer life of the people. He recognizes that the temple cannot contain God, since even heaven and the highest heaven cannot do this. Still he trusts that God's name will dwell there, and that as people turn toward this place to pray, he will hear them (cf. 27-30). He prays that the temple may become a place of just judgment for the guilty and the righteous alike (31-32). He asks that when the people are defeated in war on account of their sins, they may find forgiveness here as they implore his mercy (33-34). He also mentions rain and relief from natural disasters as gifts he asks God to grant those who pray to him in this place (35-37). Solomon extends his prayer to include every supplication made here either individually or collectively by Israelites, asking that as God knows their hearts he answer them according to all their ways (38-40). He strikes an unusual and important note when his prayer reaches out to include foreigners as well, when they come and pray toward the temple "in order that all the peoples of the earth may know thy name and fear thee" (41-43). He concludes by renewing the petition for help in battle (44-45) and for forgiveness of sins (46-50), calling to mind the choice of Israel as God's people and ending with these words: "For thou didst

8

separate them from among all the people of the earth, to be thy heritage, as thou didst bring our fathers out of Egypt, O Lord God" (v. 53). In this long and beautiful prayer Solomon expresses an understanding of God as merciful and responsive to human need and human prayer. It also expresses the center of Israel's life as the temple, and the destiny of Israel to spread the worship of God throughout the world.

Jeremiah: Prayer in Affliction
Prophets almost by definition are men of prayer, for prophetic inspiration involved a strong sense of the presence and action of God, and a spontaneous response to this, which is itself a prayer of some sort. Jeremiah's prophetic career coincided with the final years of Jerusalem, before the Babylonian King Nebuchadnezzar, who had subdued the city several times, finally tore down its walls and destroyed the temple. To prophesy in these circumstances was a source of great personal anguish to Jeremiah, an anguish he gives voice to many times. God's determination to punish and purify his people is made clear to the prophet in words strongly reminiscent of God's requesting Moses to let him alone so he could destroy the people in the desert; he directs Jeremiah several times not to pray for the city and its inhabitants: "As for you, do not pray for this people, or lift up cry or prayer for them, and do not intercede with me, for I do not hear you" (Jer. 7.16; cf. 11.14, 14.11). Nevertheless, Jeremiah prays for the defeat of Israel's enemies (10.25), and inspires prayers of repentance (14.7-9) acknowledging the power of God over nature (14.19-22) and human life (17.12-13). When the first of Jerusalem's citizens were sent as captives to Babylon, Jeremiah sent them a letter warning them that their captivity would be long and urging them to settle down to life in Babylon, and even to pray for that city "for in its welfare you will find your welfare" (Jer. 29.7). This is the only place in the Old

9

Testament where prayer for one's enemies is taught, even though the motivation is somewhat self-regarding. He tells the captives that after seventy years, in response to their prayers (29.11-14), God will keep his promise and restore them to the city of Jerusalem. As time wore on, the people remaining in Jerusalem were afflicted by wars and political turmoil. There was a movement to leave the land of Judah and go to Egypt. The people asked Jeremiah to pray to the Lord and ask Him to show them what to do (cf. 37.3; 42.2). He agrees and devotes himself to prayer for ten days. At the end, he tells them that God is willing to have mercy on them and to build them up, provided they are willing to remain in their own land and not go through with their plans to escape to Egypt (42.7-21). But they turn on him, refuse to believe him, and take him with them into Egypt.

Jeremiah's experience with prayer makes clear the meaning of calling upon God in times of trouble. He is not an automatic source of wish-fulfillment. He answers these prayers, not by responding favorably to the selfish wishes of unrepentant hearts, but by summoning to repentance, by predicting the inevitable results of deserting him, and by promising the fruits of his mercy to a purified and converted people. God's patience is inexhaustible. If they will return now, he will receive them now. But he is prepared to wait several generations until they turn back to him, then he will rebuild their city and their nation.

Judith: Triumph through Prayer
The Book of Judith is a short story set in the time of the Assyrian invasions. Judith herself is a noble Jewish woman who slays Holofernes, the Assyrian general, second in power only to the king himself. Her name means "Jewess," and in her confidence in God she personifies the whole people. The event itself is fictional, but the truth it conveys about the relationship between

God and his people is real, a truth made clear by the centuries of Israel's struggles with her enemies. Once Judith has determined on her plan to get into the Assyrian general's tent, she prays to God for help in words that distill much of Israel's faith in God. She appeals to his almighty creative power and to the covenant that binds Israel to him as his own people (cf. Jdt. 9). The events themselves unfold with the tenseness and excitement generated by a real storyteller. When the deed is done, and Judith has brought the head of Holofernes to the Israelite camp, she raises a song of praise to God. Once again she celebrates his power over nature and history, and she recalls his unfailing help to Israel, the people of the covenant (cf. Jdt. 16). Although the event is fictional, and although the Book of Judith is not included in the Hebrew canon of sacred writings (it is part of the Catholic canon, however), the story made such an impression on popular piety and imagination, that the triumph of Judith over Holofernes came to be celebrated annually in the Jewish liturgy at the feast of Hanukkah.

SOME GENERAL CONCLUSIONS
ABOUT OLD TESTAMENT PRAYER
Several conclusions follow from these case studies of Old Testament men and women of prayer. The first conclusion concerns the context in which all other conclusions are set: the relation of the individual and community to God established by his promise and the gift of the covenant. Every one of the cases alludes in one way or another to the personal divine initiative that God has taken in revealing himself, binding himself to them through promise, binding them to himself through covenant. From Abraham to Judith the theme is unmistakable. God has come in search of them, disclosed himself and his purposes to them; it is not they who have somehow sought him out as the creator of the universe, and discovered him by their efforts of thought and reflection. There is indeed a cosmic dimension in their

11

relationship with God; God is recognized and acknowledged as Creator of heaven and earth. But this is always announced as background, as proof of the reality of his divine power, as evidence that he is able to accomplish what he has promised and agreed to. Prayer, then, always carries this overtone of relationship to God initiated by his loving kindness and sustained by his faithfulness.

Secondly, God is addressed personally, even anthropomorphically. Their experience of God in their history led the Israelites to conceive God as one who watches over them, hears them when they cry to him, responds to their cries, their needs, and their way of acting. At times they attempt to bargain with him. Sometimes they even complain about the way he seems to be running things. But still they never reduce him to a purely human personality, differing only by reason of his greater strength. He is not capricious, or whimsical, or simply vindictive. He remains always mysterious, beyond human understanding, never to be represented in visible form however much he is like us, however true it may be that we have been made in his image and likeness.

Thirdly, Israelites in prayer expressed their dependence on God for all good things; nature, family, peace, prosperity, forgiveness, life itself all come to them from God. Miriam, Hannah, and Judith express this in different but very graphic ways. This view of God corresponds to the first part of the covenant formula, "I will be your God, and you shall be my people" (cf. Ex. 6.7; Lev. 26.12; Jer. 7.23; Ezek. 36.28). The Lord who has led them out of Egypt and made them his people through covenant, is the source of all benefits, their rock of refuge, and their sure hope for the future.

Fourthly, the second part of the covenant formula, expressing their condition as God's people, meant that cultic prayer, the praise and worship and supplication

12

voiced by the community publicly assembled, was centrally important. It was in this prayer that they realized and deepened their identity as a nation, as the people God had made his own and to whom he had given a special destiny, a unique place among the nations of the world. This aspect of their life of prayer appears in the great importance attached to the temple, the place of public worship, the sacred place toward which they prayed when they could not actually be present there. In fact, all of Israel becomes sacred as the land given by God to his people. When Naaman, the Syrian general, was healed of his leprosy by Elisha the prophet and was preparing to return to his own country, he asked that he might take with him a load of earth from Israel "for henceforth your servant will not offer burnt offering or sacrifice to any god but the Lord" (2 Kg. 5.17).

Finally, prayer was normally accompanied by an extraordinary confidence of being heard. Petition itself usually ends in thanksgiving, anticipating the favorable response that God will give to the prayer. The prayers of David and Solomon are good examples of this. The intimacy of the covenant relationship, which was likened to that between father and son (cf. Ex. 4.22) or between a mother and her infant child (cf. Is. 49.15) or between a husband and his bride (cf. Hos. 2.14-16), inspired this kind of unshakeable confidence and trust.

Chapter Two

New Testament Examples
of Persons at Prayer

From the many great examples of men and women of prayer in the New Testament we select just two at present, since many of the others will figure in what follows. The first is Mary, the Mother of Jesus, who sums up in herself the preparation of the chosen people for the coming of the Messiah, and the second is Jesus, whose life is the pattern of all Christian living.

MARY, MOTHER OF JESUS

Mary's role in the unfolding of God's saving purpose becomes clear from the words of Gabriel at the annunciation. She is to bear the one who will fulfill the promise made to David, the one indeed whose rule over Israel will be endless (cf. Lk. 1.32-33). Yet Mary's part is not just that of a physical bearer of human life; the angel greets her as "favored one" or "full of grace," one who enjoys the presence of the Lord (cf. Lk. 1.28). Her response to the angel's proposal was a prayer expressing her radical relation to God as servant or slave, and her total submission to his will as made known by the angel's message: "Behold, I am the handmaid of the Lord; let it be to me according to your word" (Lk. 1.38). In her reply she manifests the reign of God in her life.

The Prayer of Mary

Mary's prayerfulness finds its fullest expression in her hymn, the *Magnificat*, so called from the first word of its Latin form (cf. Lk. 1.46-55). This prayer falls naturally into three parts. In the first she thanks God for what has happened to her personally. These verses mingle awe and joy, gratitude and trust, humility and praise (cf. vv.

46-49). She next moves to a general consideration of how God works in history, how he shows mercy to those who fear him and need him, and how he rejects the proud and self-sufficient (vv. 50-53); here especially she reflects the spirit of Hannah's canticle, on which hers is based (cf. 1 Sam. 2.1-10). After this universal consideration Mary's prayer recalls God's faithfulness to the promises he made to the patriarchs Abraham and Israel, promises that have found their realization in what he has done in her (vv. 54-55). Throughout, Mary prays as a member of God's people, bearing their history and their expectation within her. Twice in the Lukan Infancy Gospel we encounter passages which reveal something more of Mary's interior life. In the first of these the evangelist is speaking about the shepherds' visit to the manger where the Christ child was laid, and their report concerning the angels' message. Then he adds: "But Mary kept all these things, pondering them in her heart" (Lk. 2.19). In the second, he concludes the mysterious episode of the boy Jesus in the temple by writing: "His mother kept all these things in her heart" (Lk. 2.51). These passages manifest a contemplative heart, where the words and deeds of God are treasured and their power felt. It is a dimension of a life of prayer that is indispensable for spiritual growth.

A new dimension in her prayer is opened in the episode of the marriage feast at Cana (cf. Jn. 2.1-11). Her words to Jesus on that occasion, "They have no wine," are not in themselves a prayer, much less a request for a miracle. They manifest her sympathy with the embarrassment the host is shortly to feel. They perhaps imply a hope that Jesus' resourcefulness will find some remedy for the situation. His reply to her shows that he chooses to regard her observation as a request, and he seems at first to be refusing her and pointing to a later time, after his glorification, when it will be appropriate for her to intercede with him on behalf of others: "O woman, what have you to do with me? My hour has not yet come." But once again the words do not have their obvious meaning, for Mary speaks to the servants with evident assurance that Jesus is going to do something about the situation: "Do whatever he tells you." Jesus has them fill large pots with water that he changes into wine. For John the Evangelist this is an important event, an anticipation of the hour of his glorification: "This, the first of his signs, Jesus did at Cana in Galilee, and manifested his glory; and his disciples believed in him" (Jn. 2.11). Christian piety has not failed to mark the part Mary played in this event, nor to recall the implied promise of her power of intercession with her Son in glory.

Mother of All Believers
In the Cana episode Jesus addresses Mary as "Woman," not a disrespectful title, but most unusual for a son to use in speaking with his mother. It alerts us to the fact that the relationship being considered is not simply the parental, as Jesus looks forward to the hour of his glorification. More light is cast on this when Jesus addresses his mother again as "Woman," this time in the midst of his hour while hanging on the cross (cf. Jn. 19.25-27). He says to her as she stands there with the disciple whom he loves: "Woman, behold your son!" And to him he says, "Behold, your mother!" Mary is not just the mother of Jesus, but like the first woman who is mother of all the living, she is the mother of all who believe in him. The intercession intimated at Cana is to be carried on in their behalf. Two further passages in Scripture confirm this understanding. One is the scene in the upper room as the small band of Jesus' followers await the coming of the Holy Spirit: "All these with one accord devoted themselves to prayer, together with the women and Mary the mother of Jesus, and with his brothers" (Acts 1.14). The prayer of Mary in the midst of the infant church is singled out for special mention. Much later, in the Book of Revelation the mysterious figure of the woman clothed with the sun appears (cf. Rev. 12.1-17). She is a complex personage, symbolizing

16

in the first place the people of the Old Covenant, as the bearers of the Messiah. As the mother of the Messiah, the woman is also inescapably Mary, the mother of Jesus (v. 5). She is also the mother of Jesus' followers, called here "the rest of her offspring . . . those who keep the commandments of God and bear testimony to Jesus" (v. 17). Thus, the woman is also the Church who brings us forth to life in Christ. Mary, indeed, by her unique role in the mystery of redemption, is able to symbolize both the Old and the New Israel, and to function as Mother of all believers. Her life of prayer first shown in her conversation with the angel Gabriel, comes to a special fullness in her ongoing work of intercession on behalf of the followers of Jesus, her Son. They, too, are her children.

But the prayer of Mary has meaning only in relation to Jesus and his prayer. Christians are frequently directed to offer intercessory prayer for one another (e.g., Acts 12.5; 2 Cor. 1.11; Jas. 5.16); but Jesus alone is the "Mediator between God and Man" in the fullest and strictest sense (cf. 1 Tim. 2.5; Rom. 8.34; 1 Jn. 2.1). Our prayer for one another, and the prayer of Mary and the saints on our behalf, have meaning only within the context of the prayer of Christ. It is he who gives us the example and by the gift of his Holy Spirit gives us the ability to pray. Because of its importance for our prayer and for the whole life of faith, we will examine the prayer of Jesus in some detail.

THE PRAYER OF JESUS
The memory which the Christian community preserved of the life of Jesus and enshrined in the gospel accounts was that of a man of prayer. This prayer was not peripheral or incidental to his life; it expressed rather his essential relationship to God, and provided the abiding context and inspiration of his mission. The work of his public life began at his baptism by John. Luke describes it in this way: "Now when all the people were baptized, and when Jesus also had been baptized and was pray-

17

ing, the heaven was opened, and the Holy Spirit descended upon him in bodily form, as a dove, and a voice came from heaven, 'Thou art my beloved Son; with thee I am well pleased'" (Lk. 3.21-22). The opening of the heaven, the descent of the Spirit, God's acknowledgment of him as Son, all significant for the inauguration of his messianic mission, take place as he is praying after his act of humility in being baptized by John. It is as Son of God, led, empowered, and anointed by the Spirit that Jesus carries out his task of preaching the kingdom of God, freeing captives and the oppressed, and healing the sick and maimed (cf. Lk. 4.1, 14, 18). Immediately after his baptism the Spirit led him into the desert where he spent forty days fasting and praying, thus recalling the example of Moses and Elijah (cf. Dt. 9.9; 1 Kg. 19.8), and the forty-year sojourn of the Hebrew people in the desert.

Thereafter, a life of intense preaching and healing began which attracted much attention. Luke gives a brief summary: "The report went abroad concerning him; and great multitudes gathered to hear and to be healed of their infirmities" (Lk. 5.15). But in the midst of all this, Jesus found time to pray: "But he withdrew to the wilderness and prayed" (Lk. 5.16). Some indication of how he did this is given by Mark. One day in Capernaum Jesus had preached in the synagogue. He went then to Simon's home, where he healed the disciple's mother-in-law. Later that evening he healed many sick with various diseases and cast out demons. The next morning, "a great while before day, he rose and went out to a lonely place, and there he prayed." His apostles found him there, and he set off once more to preach and to heal (cf. Mk. 1.21-39).

Special Occasions of Prayer
Besides this, which we may regard as Jesus' habitual practice, there were special occasions of prayer. Before he chose the twelve, a moment of great importance for the realization of his mission, Luke tells us, "he went

out to the mountain to pray; and all night he continued in prayer to God. And when it was day, he called his disciples, and chose from them twelve, whom he named apostles" (Lk. 6.12-13). After they had been with him for some time, hearing his words and seeing his deeds of kindness and power, he had an important question to ask them. Luke relates: "Now it happened that as he was praying alone the disciples were with him; and he asked them, 'Who do the people say that I am?'" To this first question they gave various answers: John the Baptist, Elijah, some other prophet risen from the dead. But then he places the question for which he had prepared by prayer: "But who do you say I am?" Peter answered for them all by saying, "The Christ of God" (cf. Lk. 9.18-20). Matthew amplifies Peter's answer: "The Christ, the Son of the Living God." Jesus expressed his satisfaction with this answer by declaring Simon blessed, for this knowledge had come to him, not from any human source, but by a revelation of the Father (cf. Mt. 16.16-17).

Jesus and the Father
On another occasion, giving thanks for the way the Father was making the kingdom known, Jesus offered a prayer which is the first prayer of Jesus for which the gospels give us the words: "I thank thee, Father, Lord of heaven and earth, that thou hast hidden these things from the wise and understanding and revealed them to babes; yea, Father, for such was thy gracious will" (Mt. 11.25-26; Lk. 10.21). What is most significant about this prayer is the name by which Jesus addresses God, "Father!" Joachim Jeremias has shown both that this was an actual historical usage of Jesus and that it was altogether new.[1] The original Aramaic is "Abba," preserved for us in several New Testament passages (Mk. 14.36; Rom. 8.15; Gal. 4.6). It was the way a child addressed its father, both while very young and into adulthood. It had overtones of familiarity and intimacy, conveyed in English to some extent by a word like "Daddy" or "Papa." Jeremias observes: "Jesus' use of

abba in addressing God reveals the heart of his relationship with God."[2] The depths and uniqueness of this relationship can be perceived in the words of explanation attributed to Jesus immediately following the prayer: "All things have been delivered to me by my Father; and no one knows the Son except the Father, and no one knows the Father except the Son and any one to whom the Son chooses to reveal him" (Mt. 11.27). A unique relationship of mutual knowledge is here affirmed, a relationship in which Jesus is simply designated as "the Son" in relation to God, who is called "the Father" in relation to Jesus. Jeremias sees in these references to God as his Father "the central statement of Jesus' mission."[3]

The Bread of Life
Before the multiplication of the loaves and fishes Jesus gave thanks and blessed the food in keeping with Jewish prayers before eating (cf. Mt. 14.19; 15.36; Mk. 6.41; 8.6, 7; Lk. 9.16; Jn. 6.11). But on one of these occasions after feeding thousands in the wilderness Jesus went up a mountain by himself and spent the night in prayer once again (cf. Mk. 6.46; Mt. 14.22-23; Jn. 6.15). This night of prayer preceded the great sermon on the Bread of Life when Jesus was to call for faith in himself and his mission. As a result of that call many turned away. But at Jesus' inquiry whether the twelve would also go away, Peter again made a profession of faith for all of them: "Lord, to whom shall we go? You have the words of eternal life; and we have believed, and have come to know that you are the Holy One of God" (Jn. 6.68-69).

As the opposition to Jesus grew and his life began to turn toward its consummation in Jerusalem, he again climbed a mountain with three of his apostles to pray and to prepare them for what was to come; this was the occasion of the Transfiguration (cf. Lk. 9.28-36). As Peter, James, and John looked on "and as he was praying, the appearance of his countenance was altered, and his raiment became dazzling white" (Lk. 9.29). Moses and Elijah, representing the law and the prophets, appeared and spoke with him about the departure (the Greek is the word for *exodus*) he will shortly accomplish in Jerusalem. The Father again made his voice heard as at the baptism: "This is my Son, my Chosen; listen to him!" At this turning point in his life, while he was praying, the Father reaffirmed his love for his Son who was preparing for the supreme manifestation of his mission and role as Son in obedience even unto death.

"Lord, teach us to pray"
In Luke's account it is on this journey to Jerusalem that the attractiveness of Jesus' prayer caused his disciples to ask him: "Lord, teach us to pray, as John taught his disciples" (Lk. 11.1). Jesus then taught them the Lord's Prayer, the central model of Christian prayers. In it he directed his followers also to address God as *abba*, "dear Father," or "Daddy." Jeremias sees in this, testimony to the new relationship with God we have through the gift of his Son. "For them [Jesus' followers] the privilege of repeating Jesus' 'Abba' amounted to an anticipation of the fulfillment of the promise: 'I will be your father, and you will be my sons and daughters' (II Cor. 6:18=II Sam. 7:14, free quotation)."[4] This is the essential relationship of the new covenant.

Toward the end of his public life, as he is near or in the city of Jerusalem, Jesus offers prayers on four different occasions, three times for others, once for himself. The first was for little children, whose mothers brought them to him that "he might lay his hands on them and pray" (Mt. 19.13). The apostles objected, seeking probably to protect Jesus from their importunity. But Jesus overrode their objections, saying that the Kingdom of God belongs to such as these. "And he took them in his arms and blessed them, laying hands upon them" (Mk. 10.16). On another occasion, before Jesus called Lazarus from the tomb, he prayed in gratitude to God: "Father, I thank thee, that thou hast heard me. I knew that thou

21

hearest me always, but I have said this on account of the people standing by, that they may believe that thou didst send me" (Jn. 11.41-42). On his last day in the temple, as he anticipated the struggle to come, Jesus spoke in anguish, "Now is my soul troubled." He asked whether he was to pray, "Father, save me from this hour." And he replied, "No, for this purpose I have come to this hour." Then he made his prayer of submission: "Father, glorify thy name" (cf. Jn. 12.27-28a). It is the first petition he taught his followers to make in praying the "Our Father." And the evangelist tells us that a voice from heaven answered Jesus' prayer: "I have glorified it, and I will glorify it again" (Jn. 12.28b). The last of these four prayers Jesus disclosed at the Last Supper, as he spoke to Simon: "Simon, Simon, behold, Satan demanded to have you, that he might sift you like wheat." According to the Greek text, Jesus here used a plural form "you" to indicate that all the apostles were involved in Satan's plans. Jesus continued in the singular, indicating Simon Peter's future role: "But I have prayed for you that your faith may not fail; and when you have turned again, strenghthen your brethren (cf. Lk. 22.31-32).

The Passion and Death of Jesus
During the final hours of his life Jesus prayed frequently. At the Last Supper, besides the ritual prayers prescribed for the passover feast, he offered his so-called high priestly prayer (cf. Jn. 17.1-26). This is a long and rich passage, reflecting the years of meditation and reflection of the evangelist as he looked back to that time and place. Jesus prayed first for himself, for his own glorification that he might fulfill his mission of glorifying the Father. Jesus' glorification is found in the manifestation of his sonship through the perfect obedience to his Father in accepting death on the cross, and through being raised from death in the Father's acceptance of Jesus' self-giving. He prayed also for the apostles, that

22

God would keep them in his name, keep them from evil, unite and sanctify them for the mission that Jesus confided to them. Finally, he prayed also for his future followers and believers in him, for their unity, and for their sharing in his glory by being also the children of the Father. This unity and glory is to be such as to bear witness to the truth of Jesus' mission. He prays also for their final union with him in glory, the Father's love in them, as he too dwells in them.

Later, in the garden, Jesus again prayed as Son of God. He revealed the immensity of the struggle he faced as he prayed for the removal of the cup; but his prayer ended on the note of perfect submission: "Abba, Father, all things are possible to thee; remove this cup from me; yet not what I will, but what thou wilt" (Mk. 14.36). This, too, is a petition from the "Our Father." The Letter to the Hebrews, in evident reference to this scene, says: "In the days of his flesh, Jesus offered up prayers and supplications, with loud cries and tears, to him who was able to save him from death, and he was heard for his godly fear" (Heb. 5.7). The Father heard Jesus' prayers, not by preventing his death, but by raising him from the dead.

Three different prayers are attributed to Jesus as he hung upon the cross. The first of these is a prayer for his persecutors, that the Father would forgive them since they act out of ignorance: "Father, forgive them, for they know not what they do" (Lk. 23.34). Jesus here fulfilled the command he had given in the Sermon on the Mount: "Love your enemies, and pray for those who persecute you, so that you may be sons of your Father who is in heaven" (Mt. 5.44-45a). St. Paul recalls, too, the ignorance of those who crucified Jesus, when he writes: "None of the rulers of this age understood this [wisdom]; for if they had, they would not have crucified the Lord of glory" (1 Cor. 2.8).

The other two prayers of Jesus on the cross are both taken from psalms. The first is the opening of Psalm 22: "My God, my God, why hast thou forsaken me?" (Mk. 15.34; Mt. 27.46). This is the only prayer of Jesus in which he does not address God as Father. This may be because the psalm itself provides the mode of address, but it also is no doubt due to the utter loneliness and desolation of that hour which overwhelmed the feelings of intimacy and caring suggested by the word Father. Jesus knew the psalm began in a mood of utter abandonment, which corresponded to his own, but that it moved toward a conclusion of trust and divine triumph. There is no reason to suppose he did not intend the whole meaning of the psalm.

The final prayer of Jesus is given by Luke: "Father, into thy hands I commit my spirit" (Lk. 23.46). Except for the title Father, this is taken from Ps. 31.5. It is a psalm of trust amid great afflictions and difficulties. A little later on the psalmist prays: "Be gracious to me, O Lord, for I am in distress; my eye is wasted from grief, my soul and my body also. For my life is spent with sorrow, and my years with sighing; my strength fails because of my misery, and my bones waste away" (Ps. 31.9-10). This too mirrors Jesus' feeling and condition. In this moment, as Son he fulfills the Father's will to the uttermost, refusing either to back down before threats and torments or to respond in kind. To the end he manifests the unconditioned love of the Father for sinful humanity. The words of the First Letter of Peter are a fitting commentary on this final prayer of Jesus: "He committed no sin; no guile was found on his lips. When he was reviled, he did not revile in return; when he suffered, he did not threaten; but he trusted to him who judges justly" (1 Pet. 2.22-23).

Jesus' Prayer in Glory
In the perspective of the New Testament, Jesus' life of prayer did not end with his death, but continues now on

our behalf. This thought is represented in different ways in almost every strand of New Testament tradition. St. Paul speaks about Jesus as the one "who died, yes, who was raised from the dead, who is at the right hand of God, who indeed intercedes for us" (Rom. 8.34). The Letter to the Hebrews says, "He is able for all time to save those who draw near to God through him, since he always lives to make intercession for them" (Heb. 7.25). The First Letter of John reminds us, "If any one sins, we have an advocate with the Father, Jesus Christ the righteous" (1 Jn. 2. 1). It is because Jesus unites himself with our prayers that they are efficacious, as we learn from the Gospel according to Matthew: "If two of you agree on earth about anything they ask, it will be done for them by my Father in heaven. For where two or three are gathered in my name, there am I in the midst of them" (Mt. 18.19-20). Finally, the gift of the Holy Spirit comes to us through the prayers of Jesus, as we learn from the Gospel according to John: "I will pray the Father, and he will give you another Counselor, to be with you for ever, even the Spirit of truth" (Jn. 14.16-17a).

CONCLUSIONS CONCERNING PRAYER
IN THE NEW TESTAMENT
We will conclude by making some general observations about the prayer of Jesus, then noting how this prayer manifests the personality of Jesus, and finally drawing some conclusions from the prayer of Jesus and Mary as applicable to the prayer of Christians in general.

The New Testament description of Jesus' prayer makes it clear that this kind of communion with God was frequent and habitual throughout his life, even when he was busily occupied with preaching and healing. It was not just a question of his finding time to squeeze it in somehow; rather prayer belonged to the essence of his life and mission. Praying was simply an integral part of the whole matter of living for him. This prayer assumed

25

many forms, depending on the circumstances of his life. There were prayers of praise, gratitude, submission, and trust. There were petitions for himself and for others. Before the great events of his mission there were special prayers that sometimes took most or all of the night; we may recall the prayer before the choice of the twelve, before the sermon on the bread of life, and before the apostles' profession of faith, the raising of Lazarus, and His own suffering and death. Jesus constantly employed a new and even revolutionary way of addressing God; he called him "Abba"—which we may translate as "dear Father" or "Daddy" or "Papa"— expressing an unheard of sense of familiarity and intimacy.

People manifest and even constitute their personalities in the way they relate to other persons. For Jesus it is true to say that his personality is essentially constituted by his relationship to God as his Father, a relationship that found its constant expression in his life of prayer. Jesus is before all else the Son in his relationship to God and this shapes his relationship to all other persons. Jesus shows himself humble and dependent on God in prayer, with a humility and dependence that is all-pervasive. His prayer thus shows him to be completely obedient to the Father's will, spontaneously grateful for the Father's gifts, full of praise for the Father's deeds, completely trusting in the Father's disposition of his life, intent on carrying out the mission given him by the Father, and closely united with his Father in thought, purpose, sentiment, and affection. This intimate relationship with God in turn determines how he relates to other persons. He bears within himself the purpose and the love of God for others, and thus his prayer shows care, concern, forgiveness, and acceptance of his fellow human beings. At the same time he is strong and authoritative in revealing to them the truth of their condition before God and of God's abiding love for them. His prayer shows him able to draw upon the divine power for their relief and well-being. The prayerfulness of Jesus drew others to him, to ask him to teach them how to pray, and to bless and pray for their children. The prayerfulness of Jesus is an important part of the attractiveness of his personality.

Continuity Between Old and New Testaments
The prayer of Jesus and Mary that we have considered leads to some important conclusions about the New Testament view of prayer for all Christians. There is, first of all, a profound continuity between the Old and the New Testament teaching on prayer. The conclusions we drew at the end of the first chapter continue to be true, but their full meaning is to be seen only in the light of the person and prayer of Jesus. Prayer continues to be the fruit of a divine initiative, a response to the God who has first loved us, sent his Son into the world that we should live through him, and given us the Holy Spirit as the pledge of our redemption. We pray within the context of a New Covenant which joins us to God by giving us a share in Jesus' own relationship to God as Father.

The God to whom we turn in prayer is the same personal God revealed in the Old Testament, but now known as the Father of our Lord Jesus Christ, and as our Father also, through our relation to Jesus Christ. Through the gift of his Spirit we too call out "Abba! dear Father!" It is not just that the people as a whole are personified as "the son of God," but each of us in our relationship to God discovers that individually we are his children, each of us his son or daughter. We pray to one who knows us intimately, loves us endlessly, cares for us personally, and calls us to life in himself, forgiving our sins and healing all our ills.

Our Father, as in the Old Testament, is also for us in the New Testament the source of all good. The covenant formula is not only: "I will be their God and they shall

27

be my people"; it is also: "I shall be a Father to you and you shall be my sons and daughters" (cf. 2 Cor. 6.18). He became our Father by delivering up his Son who faithfully manifested the Father's love even unto death. St. Paul asks, "Will he not also give us all things with him?" (Rom. 8.32). In the prayer that Jesus taught us to say to him, we learn that our Father is the source of daily bread, forgiveness of sins, and deliverance from ultimate trial and evil.

Prayer in the New Testament also has a social aspect. It manifests and forms us as the family of God, his sons and daughters. In the prayer that Jesus taught us to say, all the petitions are made in the plural for *us*, not simply for me; and God is addressed (in the Matthean form) as *our* Father (cf. Mt. 6.9). After the example of Jesus and following his teaching, we are to pray for one another, even for our enemies. The prayer of Mary speaks to us of the communion of saints, our fellowship with those who have died and are now with Christ; their prayers on our behalf are rooted in the unity of the one Spirit who binds all together in the Body of Christ, and draw their power and acceptability before God from the same source. The prayers of all believers, whether living or dead, are made with Jesus, who is present wherever any gather and pray in his name, and through Jesus, who intercedes for us, and in Jesus, whose Body we are through the gift of his life-giving Spirit.

Finally, the prayer of the New Testament, relying on the promises and the prayers of Jesus, is made with great confidence. This prayer is an all-pervasive element of Christian life, looking to the past with gratitude and praise, to the present with peace and joy, to the future with trust and assured hope. Christian prayer is always a response to the eternal and loving initiative of God the Father, which has been made visible to us through the life, death, and resurrection of Jesus Christ, his Son, and has been communicated to us by his Holy Spirit. Our response to this initiative is likewise inspired by the grace of the Holy Spirit dwelling in us, and is joined to the unceasing prayer of Jesus our Mediator, and thus unfailingly finds an acceptable hearing with the Father.

The conclusions we have set down, based on the example of great men and women of prayer in the Old and New Testament, still leave us with the kinds of questions that were raised in the introduction. How can anyone in this present scientific and technological age entertain ideas like these except through some kind of poetic fantasy? In the following chapters we want to specify more clearly some of these questions and to propose answers to them. The first question, to be dealt with in the following chapter, raises the old biblical problem: "Where is your God?" Prayer supposes that God is somehow present and acting in our world. It is the most basic presupposition of the whole enterprise of praying, and perhaps the most difficult to deal with satisfactorily from our contemporary mind set.

NOTES

1. Joachim Jeremias, *Prayers of Jesus*, Studies in Biblical Theology, second series, n. 6 (Naperville, Ill.: Alec R. Allenson, Inc., 1967), pp. 54-65.

2. Ibid., p. 62.

3. Ibid., p. 53.

4. Ibid., p. 64.

Chapter Three

"Where is your God?"

For a religious person there can be scarcely any area of inquiry more important than the one which John Courtney Murray called the "existential" question: "The existential question is whether God is here with us now. The word 'existential' bears a biblical sense, referring to the active existence of God in history, his presence in the midst of his people."[1] For the theology of prayer it is clearly radically important. For prayer, however we may finally define it, involves some kind of relationship with God. If we cannot conceive or imagine this relationship in a realistic way, not simply as some kind of metaphor, prayer is finally impossible. We may then reword the question, "Where is your God?" to read, "Where is God actively present in relation to us?"

UNSATISFACTORY ANSWERS
In trying to reply to this question we will first note two unsatisfactory answers that have often been given, based on a somewhat superficial reading of Scripture. Next we will try to get a better grasp of the biblical response. Finally, we will venture an answer that draws upon philosophical reflection guided by the perspective of biblical faith.

God Located in a Sacred Place
The first of these unsatisfactory answers simply locates God in a sacred place, like the temple at Jerusalem. Psalm 42, for example, could be cited in favor of this view; it begins with a sense of the absence of God: "As a hart longs for flowing streams, so longs my soul for

thee, O God." The mood continues and is reinforced at the end of the third verse with a question that the psalmist's enemies put to him: "Where is your God?" The question is a taunt, pointing to the affliction of the psalmist as evidence of the impotence and absence of the God he worships. But the psalm continues with reminiscence, hope, encouragement, and finally comes to a prayer: "Oh send out thy light and thy truth; let them lead me, let them bring me to thy holy hill and to thy dwelling" (Ps. 43.3).[2] The holy hill is Mount Zion in Jerusalem; God's dwelling is the temple. Similar references can be found in other places. For example, Psalm 46.4 reads: "There is a river whose streams make glad the city of God, the holy habitation of the Most High." Psalm 84 begins: "How lovely is thy dwelling place, O Lord of hosts! My soul longs, yea, faints for the courts of the Lord." And in Psalm 132, a Song of Ascents sung by pilgrims on the way to Jerusalem, verse 7 exhorts: "Let us go to his dwelling place; let us worship at his footstool!"

It is possible to mistake the mood and meaning of these passages. Of themselves they simply point to the place of ritual thanksgiving, the place where God is honored, a place which symbolizes God's presence in the midst of his people. They are not intended to restrict the presence of God, to limit the sphere of his effective action. But it is easy to think of sacred places as those where God is present, and other places as those where he is not. These other places are "profane" (derived from the Latin *pro* and *fanum*, meaning before or outside the shrine).

A later age, continuing the distinction between the sacred and the profane, sought in a somewhat more sophisticated fashion to locate the presence of God. He would be found, they reasoned, in those places where we encounter the inexplicable. If something happens for which no other explanation can be found, we may say that this is the locus of the divine action and so, God supposedly inhabits the gaps where our powers of enquiry and explanation falter before the mystery of the universe. God conceived in this way has been called the God of the gaps. These gaps vary depending on the degree of scientific development. At one time astronomy books unquestioningly assumed that God took care of certain tasks in the universe: he kept the fixed stars from falling together under the constant pull of universal gravitation; he confined the somewhat erratic motions of the planets within fixed limits; he guaranteed the continuous supply of solar energy, etc. It is told that in 1796 when Laplace presented his great work on the motion of the planets to his friend Napoleon, the future emperor looked through it, and then made the puzzled observation, "But you say nothing about God." To this the astronomer replied, "I have no need of that hypothesis." More recently it was maintained that only a special divine intervention could explain the emergence of life from the nonliving, sterile matter of the world in its primordial condition. But gradually, as these areas become explicable, at least in great measure, God is made to retreat from the gaps marked out by our ignorance. Finally, there is no such temple for God to dwell in. The whole universe becomes profane. Clearly, the answer to the question, "Where is your God?" cannot be given in terms of certain select places.

God Located in the Heavens
A second unsatisfactory answer, one that also relies upon an inadequate interpretation of Scripture, locates God in a place of transcendent height. Psalm 115 contrasts the Israelites with the idolatrous Gentiles who surround them. These point to their own gods of silver and gold, and jeer at the Israelites with the question, "Where is their God?" (Ps. 115.2). The psalm replies at once, "Our God is in the heavens; he does whatever he pleases" (v. 3), and proceeds to contrast this tran-

scendent and all-powerful God with the dead, inert, helpless gods of the Gentiles. This reference to the heavens as God's abode is fairly common. For example, Psalm 2.4 simply describes God as "He who sits in the heavens." Psalm 123 begins, "To thee I lift up my eyes, O thou who art enthroned in the heavens!"

Once again, the Hebrew usage is symbolic, not realistic or scientific. But it is easy to pass from an apt symbolism to a mistaken realism. The blue dome that appears to overarch the earth, the firmament in which the sun and moon and stars are fixed, is a spontaneous and natural symbol of transcendence, of that which is beyond and above mere human experience and day-to-day life. God may be thought of as abiding there, unchangeably constant in his oversight of the world and his care for all things. The Ptolemaic system of astronomy, developed by the Greco-Egyptian Claudius Ptolemy in the second century of the Christian era and reflecting a view of the world advanced by Greek philosophy centuries before, conceived the universe as a series of concentric spheres revolving about the earth. The lower spheres were moved by the higher spheres. The highest sphere, known as the empyrean, was moved directly by God, whose influence thus reached all of creation. This theory persisted into the sixteenth century, when it was challenged by Copernicus and Galileo. Even though it was not advanced as a total explanation of God's activity in the world, it exercised strong influence on the popular imagination, and it was easy to think of God as "out beyond the shining of the farthest star," in the words of a nineteenth-century hymn.

Whatever imaginative and emotional symbolic value the heavens may retain today as an abode of God, the symbolism itself is basically inadequate. For transcendence then becomes understood as distance and remoteness. God is thought of as occupying some divine realm infinitely separated from our world, and then acting in the

33

world from time to time in miracles or revelations or in answer to prayers. But, for many people at least, it is impossible to make much sense out of such transcendent locations.

THE ANSWER OF SCRIPTURE
The biblical response to our enquiry into the presence and activity of God is far richer than what has been suggested about sacred places and transcendent abodes. The Scriptures explicitly teach the inadequacy of such ideas. Solomon, at the dedication of the temple, offered this prayer: "But will God indeed dwell on earth? Behold, heaven and the highest heaven cannot contain thee; how much less this house which I have built?" (1 Kg. 8.27). There is simply no place that can contain God or restrict his presence. This leads to reflections on the divine omnipresence, God's presence everywhere. Jeremiah points out how the false prophets cannot evade God: "Am I a God at hand, says the Lord, and not a God afar off? Can a man hide himself in secret places so that I cannot see him? says the Lord. Do not I fill heaven and earth? says the Lord" (Jer. 23.23-24). Psalm 139 recalls that wherever one might flee, God is there:

Whither shall I go from thy Spirit?
    Or whither shall I flee from thy presence?
If I ascend to heaven, thou art there!
    If I make my bed in Sheol, thou art there!
If I take the wings of the morning
    and dwell in the uttermost parts of the sea,
even there thy hand shall lead me,
    and thy right hand shall hold me.   (vv. 7-10)

From Him, through Him, in Him
Several places in the New Testament indicate our relationship to God through the use of prepositions. This begins to tell us where we should look to find him, along what lines we should set our sights. Paul's speech

in the Areopagus at Athens tells how God distributed the human race throughout the earth, "that they should seek God, in the hope that they might feel after him and find him. Yet he is not far from each one of us for 'in him we live and move and have our being'; as even some of your poets have said, 'For we are indeed his offspring'" (Acts. 17.27-28). This says that we are *in* God, and hence he is close to each of us. The meaning of this *in* seems to be indicated just before this, where God is said to give us "life and breath and everything" (v. 25). God surrounds and supports us as the nurturing source of all we have and are and do. But we are not told how we are to understand this, how we may conceive God at work in the world.

In an even more comprehensive description of the relation of the world to God, Paul writes: "For from him and through him and to him are all things. To him be glory for ever. Amen" (Rom. 11.36). This is the cosmic context of dependence on God, in which Paul locates the history of salvation. *From him* points to God as the creative source of all reality. *Through him*, like *in him* in the speech at the Areopagus, refers to God as the sustainer and support of the universe. *To him* points to God as the end and goal of creation.[3]

The New Testament has one other special point of view that needs to be noted. It is especially strong in Johannine writings: "If we love one another, God abides in us. . . . Whoever confesses that Jesus is the Son of God, God abides in him and he in God. . . . God is love, and he who abides in love, abides in God and God abides in him" (1 Jn. 4. 12, 15, 16). Love and faith are intimate sharings in the life of God, so that there is a mutual indwelling between God and the one in whom these are truly operative.

These passages from the Scriptures do not confine God to any special location in response to our question about his presence and action in the world. They don't allow us to pin him down, but they direct our attention beyond sacred places and gaps and symbolic distances to the totality of the world, to the origin and ground and goal of all things. But how are we to think these things today? How does our awareness and self-understanding and world view enable us to make sense of this and somehow face toward him? Where can we think of his almighty power actually working in the world?

BASIC INSIGHTS OF THEOLOGY AND PHILOSOPHY
Recent theology has, of course, been concerned with these questions. A movement of great significance for reading and understanding the Bible laid great importance on the whole development of history as recorded there. They spoke of salvation history or, to use the German word, *Heilsgeschichte*. A recurrent theme was "the great deeds of God."[4] But this movement encountered a problem: what is God doing in history? What can we point to and say this is God's doing? If God is acting, what is he doing that is not being done by some more obvious and visible agents? As Langdon Gilkey has written about this question: "That activity [of God] was 'there,' and 'real,' but it was to be seen only by faith. Where that 'there' was, if it was *not* in observable natural or human history, and still more *not* in some Greek eternity was thus left a problem which hounded Biblical theology almost to its death."[5]

God as the "Ground of Being"
Some of the most fruitful thinking about the presence and action of God in the world was initiated by Paul Tillich, who spoke of God as "the ground of being."[6] His approach led many people to look at the interior dimension of things as the locus of divine presence. Thus John A. T. Robinson, in his immensely popular book, *Honest to God*, entitled his pivotal chapter, "The Ground of Our Being."[7] In it he wrote: "God, the un-

36

conditional, is to be found only in, with *and under* the conditioned relationships of this life: for he *is* their depth and ultimate significance."[8] Gregory Baum, who was probably not directly influenced by Paul Tillich in this matter, nevertheless wrote about the popular view of God as "the supreme being and king of the universe": "Does this outsider God exist at all?"[9]

In spite of the strongly ontological tone of some of these remarks, the approach was more ontic or existential than ontological. That is, it concentrated on human experience and interpersonal relationships rather than on the being of the universe in general. Thus, Gregory Baum wrote: "The locus of the divine is the interpersonal. God is present in that area of human life where man, in fact, invests most of his intellectual and emotional energies, namely his ordinary, secular existence. We may summarize these remarks by saying that God is the mystery of man's humanization."[10] But human existence must be seen against the background of the universe. Langdon Gilkey, referring to the philosophical efforts of early Christianity, speaks of our need today in this way:

"The same requirement that theology be 'ontological' as well as 'ontic,' so that its language about God, the world, and man achieve the necessary universality and permanence to transcend the immediate structures of being, is present today as it was in the first five centuries—lest again God be a being less than ultimate, and lest his promises be a mere palliative in a world beyond his own final control."[11]

Faith and Speculation
The need which Gilkey indicates for an ontological treatment of this question points to a different methodology than that of biblical research. The faith of the Bible offers us the answer we require but does not provide us with a contemporary understanding of it.

37

Besides the imaginative and experiential answer of the sacred writers we need a kind of speculative and rational answer which will make the biblical answer acceptable to our modern mentality. This speculative and rational answer has certain severe limitations about it, most notably that it is not of itself religious. It does not by itself spell out the personal love and concern of God for us that lies back of his presence and action in the world. Yet this philosophical answer provides the context within which this love and concern can be understood to be really operative. The remaining chapters of this study on prayer will deal explicitly with the religious dimensions that philosophy tends to neglect. While the speculative answer is intended to be persuasive to the modern scientific mind, it is not a "scientific answer." While respecting and accepting scientific answers, it points out their limitations and endeavors to relate a further philosophical insight to the scientific world view.

Process Theology
A satisfactory answer to the question "Where is your God?" must then be able to integrate the existential and the ontological, that is, our personal experience of being and our knowledge of the universe around us in a way that is acceptable to the scientific viewpoint. Process theology attempts to do this, and very persuasively.[12] The God described and developed in the process philosophy of Alfred North Whitehead has some strong resemblances to the God of the Bible. He is present and active in all the events of the universe, whether human or inanimate, and he is concerned to draw all things to their highest good. But he is not the creator of the world, in the way this has been understood either in the Bible or in Christian tradition; he is himself a creature, a concrete embodiment of the creative process, having no reality apart from this process, developing and growing by his interacting relationship with the world. It seems

to me that centuries ago Christian theology suffered great damage, from which it is still recovering, by unconsciously identifying the Stoic concept of providence with the biblical understanding of God. A similar identification of the process God with the Father of our Lord Jesus Christ and the creator of heaven and earth could eventually do equal damage.[13]

A CONTEMPORARY APPROACH

In preparing a constructive answer to this question on how God is present and active in the universe I rely for an initial insight on Thomas Aquinas, for a statement of the problem and an unintended hint at a solution on Albert Einstein, and for the terms in which a solution may be framed on Teilhard de Chardin. None of these thinkers by himself provides the answer we are looking for; but together they mutually illuminate one another so that from their combined light we can offer a contemporary answer to the question, "Where is your God?"

An Initial Insight

Thomas Aquinas offers the initial insight in replying to the question whether God is in all things.[14] He replies that God is not in things as a part of their inner constitution, but in the way an agent or active principle is present to what receives its action. He cites Aristotle to the effect that a thing moving something else immediately is present to it. Since God is being itself he is the cause of the being of all things. But since nothing is more intimate to a thing than its being, for being is the actuality of all that is, God is present in all things intimately. This is highly abstract language, but it gives an initial insight as to God's active presence in the world: as the continual source of the being of all things, in things most intimately.[15]

We have already seen Einstein's primary difficulty with speaking of God as working within the universe: "For

39

him [the scientist] neither the rule of human nor the rule of divine will exists as an independent cause of natural events."[16] He is saying that the causal connections between natural bodies and events as expressed in physical laws are unbroken throughout the universe. We cannot conceive an outside will—whether human or divine—acting as another force or power alongside the physical forces and energies of matter, pushing or pulling to arrange events differently. In denying the influence of human as well as divine will Einstein is denying our reality as persons as well as the personal reality of God. He is saying that *everything* that takes place has a full and adequate explanation simply in terms of mass and energy. Nothing more is required, for nothing more is possible. "There is no room left," he says.[17]

Strange as it may seem, Einstein has done us a service by denying that the human will can influence events in a world where all natural events are causally interconnected. His objection can stimulate us to examine first of all, whether the human will in reality influences events. If it does so, then we can find in its action an analogy for understanding God's presence and action in the world, since Einstein's objection to both human and divine is the same.

Influence of the Human Will
Our consideration of the influence of the human will must be both existential and ontological; we must see both how it functions as a dimension of our own conscious existence as humans, and how it has an objectively real effect in the world around us. We are conscious of making free decisions. We choose to do one thing as we are consciously aware of our ability to do something else. These choices and decisions constitute us as the kind of persons we are, give shape and character to our personalities. This is the existential aspect of the will's activity. But our choices also affect the world

40

around us: transportation, building, communication, art, etc. all come about as the result of human choice, in a way not solely explicable in terms of material activities. Granted, these activities permeate the whole process as it takes place, but it would never take place if it were not guided and directed by the choice of the human will. Einstein once wrote a letter to President Franklin Roosevelt telling him that he thought it possible to develop an atomic bomb. Science had achieved sufficient penetration into the energies that hold matter together that it was possible to develop a technology for releasing that energy in catastrophic ways. The letter of Einstein to the president is implicit testimony to the fact that if human choice, human will, does not influence the process the atomic bomb will not come to be. In the early 1960s President John F. Kennedy set a manned trip to the moon during that decade as a goal of national endeavor. It came about, not simply as the inevitable result of various material energies at work in the world, but as the fruit of many human decisions operating to guide and direct those energies. There would have been no trip from earth to moon, whether manned or unmanned, if human wills had not chosen that it take place. It is clear that human choice does not itself provide the energy which it influences or controls; but somehow it determines the way that energy is to be expended.

Will and Body
The central feature of the influence of the human will upon the external world is its influence upon the human body. Our choices influence the world because they influence the motions of our body, the expenditure of the energy we derive from eating and breathing. How are we to regard this influence of the will over our bodily activities? Some would reply it is merely a delusion, born of our ignorance as to what really is impelling us to act. We don't know what makes us act, and thus we are led to imagine that we ourselves make the free decision to act

41

in one way or another. Delusion as an explanation is not only purely gratuitous, it also neglects the fact that we can very sharply distinguish between those actions over which we can exercise some control and those we cannot, though we recognize we ourselves are doing both of them. I can choose whether or not to shave; I cannot control the growth of hair on my face. I can choose whether or not to open my eyes or to look at something; I cannot control what I see if I choose to look. I can choose whether to eat something or not; I have very little control over the process of digestion which follows. I can choose to go for a run; I cannot control the speed of my heartbeat if I do. It is manifestly and immediately evident to us that our choices do significantly affect much of what we do, as evident as any data that can be discovered through laboratory experiment, and hence not to be overturned by such data.

Choice
Choice, however, is experienced neither as the inevitable result of previous biochemical states nor as the source of some kind of force or energy for what we do. If I have decided on a routine of regular exercise, I recognize that as time approaches for doing it I am free to follow out my earlier decision or not. Tiredness in my muscles or a sense of strength and energy may incline me one way or another, but neither of them determines my choice. And if I do choose to run, the firmness of my decision is no substitute for taking nourishment or breathing, both of which are necessary if I am to have energy to run.

Choice is experienced as an event within the complex unity of the human being, more specifically within what we have come to identify as the nervous system. Choice is experienced as directing the thrust of human activity toward a certain goal, in a certain direction, not by introducing a force from without, but by supplying an orientation from within. This supposes that there is in the human nervous system a certain indeterminacy, so that one state or condition does not follow as wholly determined from the previous state. It supposes that chemically and physically any one of several possible states can follow the present one. We speak of paralysis or some other disorder when this is not the case. Human choice, then, determines which of the possible states will actually follow, a state that depends upon but is not inevitably determined by the previous state. Contemporary views of the *statistical* nature of physical laws confirm this understanding of the indeterminacy of material states. A law that is statistical allows for slight variations which do not stand in contradiction to the ways matter normally acts. We ourselves experience within ourselves the indeterminacy of our nervous systems, in our capacity to determine them in different ways. Our conscious choice actually guides and determines this present state (open as it is to several possibilities) to produce the state we decide upon.

This analysis of human choice acting within the complex unity of the human nervous system proves nothing about how God is active and present in the world. But it suggests a possible approach, a way of understanding God's effective influence, which does not interfere with the network of created causes. It gives a hint of where we might look to resolve our problem. It suggests also the aptness of the terminology of Teilhard de Chardin for dealing with the matter.

The Without and the Within
Teilhard, in his analysis of matter as it is caught up in the evolutionary process leading to the appearance of the human species, makes a distinction between the 'without' and the 'within.' He reflects on the phenomenon of human consciousness, where we have a direct intuition of our own within, and concludes to the exis-

tence of a within in all material realities—not, of course, as a phenomenon of self-awareness and free choice, as it is in us, but as a dimension of inwardness, a kind of subjectivity, interiority, and depth proportionate in intensity to the development of external or organic complexity in the without. He writes:

"It is impossible to deny that, deep within ourselves, an 'interior' appears at the heart of beings, as it were seen through a rent. This is enough to ensure that, in one degree or another, this 'interior' should obtrude itself as existing everywhere in nature from all time. Since the stuff of the universe has an inner aspect at one point of itself, there is necessarily a *double aspect to its structure*, that is to say in every region of space and time—in the same way, for instance, as it is granular: *co-extensive with their Without, there is a Within to things.*"[18]

The within is set in distinction to the without, which is concerned with outwardness, physical arrangement, objectivity, exteriority, surface. The energy of the without relates material bodies to one another in different ways, depending on the degree of complexity in their structure: subatomic, atomic, molecular, and so on to greater and greater combinations of these. Science, Teilhard observes, has been concerned only with the without. "In the eyes of the physicist, nothing exists legitimately, at least up to now, except the *without* of things."[19] But we experience in ourselves, in the phenomenon of consciousness, another equally real and ultimately far more important aspect of nature: the within. The energy of the within draws together the various parts of the material body into the unity of one being; Teilhard calls it "radial energy" because it acts like radii linking all that is contained within the circumference to a center. Below the human level, consciousness is more or less attenuated; only in us does it reach sufficient intensity to have genuine centeredness: I not only know, but I know that I know; I not only wish and desire, but I will freely,

44

as the knowing cause of individual choices, consciously willing to will what I will. Consciousness has advanced so far that at the human level it takes possession of itself. And from within we influence and determine what we do in our without. This is where we had arrived in our reflections upon Einstein.

Einstein's position was to exclude the action of the human and the divine wills from interfering with the physical-chemical laws of the universe. He saw no way in which they could act directly in *the without*, that is, constitute a force similar to forces of gravity, or magnetism, or electricity. This seems not only acceptable, but absolutely necessary unless we wish to reduce the actions of the human and divine wills to material functions. But Einstein does not even raise the question of *the within*, much less does he advance evidence to exclude the human and divine wills from acting in the within of things. We ourselves recognize and experience that our wills act in the within of our beings; we thereby influence our without not as adding new external forces, but as guiding from within those which are there and operating.

God as Acting Within All Things
We have now the insights and terminology we need to answer our original question. Where is God? Where is he present and operating in the world? To this we answer, God acts in the within of all things in the universe. He is present in their within, acting to realize his purposes everywhere. Before expanding this answer somewhat, and explaining the grounds for affirming it, we may note how the Scriptures themselves in speaking of human beings employ a terminology that is very similar. Both the Old Testament and the New Testament speak of the 'heart' not usually in a physical sense as an organ of the body, but to describe the interior, the within, the seat of consciousness and feeling and choice.

Hundreds of examples of this could be given, but to note a few: "Let the words of my mouth and the meditation of my heart be acceptable in thy sight, O Lord, my rock and my redeemer" (Ps. 19.14). "Yea, our heart is glad in him, because we trust in his holy name" (Ps. 33.21). "For out of the abundance of the heart his mouth speaks" (Lk. 6.45). "It is right for me to feel thus about you all, because I hold you in my heart, for you are all partakers with me of grace" (Phil. 1.7). Paul, in particular, speaks of the *"eso anthropos"* (literally, "inner man") and sometimes contrasts this with the *"exo anthropos"* ("outer man") or some other exterior aspect. "For I delight in the law of God, in my inmost self *(kata ton eso anthropon)*, but I see in my members another law at war with the law of my mind" (Rom. 7.22-23). "So we do not lose heart. Though our outer nature is wasting away, our inner nature is being renewed every day" (2 Cor. 4.16).

But more important than the fact that Scripture notes this distinction between the within and the without at the human level, it again and again refers to God's action as precisely touching the within. "Thou hast put more joy in my heart than they have when their grain and wine abound" (Ps. 4.7). "Create in me a clean heart, O God, and put a new and right spirit within me" (Ps. 51.10). "May He grant you to be strengthened with might through his Spirit in the inner man" (Eph. 3.16). "God's love has been poured into our hearts through the Holy Spirit which has been given to us" (Rom. 5.5).

To expand, then, on the answer given above: God acts in the within of all things in the universe. Within and without are inseparable aspects of things, and in their mutual interrelatedness constitute the wholeness of these things. The within is related to the without as the principle of unity, as the support of the without's specific quality as the without of this kind of thing, as the guide or director of its activity. The without expresses the nature and intensity of the within, nourishes it, and inclines it to move in a certain direction. From the standpoint of a philosophy of being, we would say that the within communicates existence or being to the without, that the whole rests or depends ultimately on the being and reality of the within.

God's action directly touches and affects the within of each thing and of all things. He communicates to them existence, being, and reality. He does this by being the abiding source and goal of each thing in its interior dynamism. God is the beginning and the end. As the beginning God makes all things "ex-sist," that is, stand forth in the world; and as end, he is the good in whose reality all things participate. God thus energizes the world from within. He unifies each thing within itself and relates each thing to every other in the unity of one universe. He draws each and all into the future. His power and action reaches, modifies, and shapes the without by sustaining, drawing, and directing the within.

God's Transcendent Activity
There are many reasons for affirming this view of God's presence and activity. First of all, both faith and reason recognize that the world and all it contains, myself included, are dependent in being. God is said to uphold all things by the word of his power (Heb. 1.3). The phenomena of change, limitation, and contingency all manifest the fact that these things don't have to exist, but do so only in dependence on God's sustaining activity. However, we cannot understand the activity which communicates and sustains being itself as an activity of the without, as a particular kind of activity by which one thing influences another in a specific or categorical way, e.g., gravity, magnetism, heat. The activity is not categorical but transcendental, reaching everything and every aspect of everything, including the categorical activities of the without; for all these things finally share somehow in being. Hence, just as the within or center of

each thing supports its without or circumference, so God as the center of centers supports the within of all things.

Absolute Dependence on God
We may add to this the experience which Friederich Schleiermacher called the "feeling of absolute dependence." He regarded this as the third and highest state of conscious awareness. A person begins in a state of confusion, not clearly distinguishing between oneself and the surrounding world. A second stage supervenes in which one realizes this distinction by the experience of a limited dependence and independence with regard to the things around one. It is possible to control them to some degree, and hence to be somewhat independent, but at the same time they exercise some control and hence render one dependent. This distinction between oneself and the world is caught up into a higher unity as at a third level one comes to realize, "feel," experience that the whole is absolutely dependent, that all things together are dependent on God.[20]

Teilhard de Chardin describes this experience in a very compelling paragraph:

"And so, for the first time in life perhaps (although I am supposed to meditate every day!), I took the lamp and, leaving the zone of everyday occupations and relationships where everything seems clear, I went down into my inmost self, to the deep abyss whence I feel dimly that my power of action emanates. But as I moved further and further away from the conventional certainties by which social life is superficially illuminated, I became aware that I was losing contact with myself. At each step of the descent a new person was disclosed within me of whose name I was no longer sure, and who no longer obeyed me. And when I had to stop my exploration because the path faded from beneath my steps, I found a bottomless abyss at my feet, and out of

48

it came—arising I know not from where—the current which I dare to call *my* life."[21]

Meaning of God's Presence and Activity in Things
We need to make two points very clear when we say that God is everywhere present and active in the within of things. first, he is not to be *identified* with the within of things. We cannot say that God *is* the within of things, their deepest dimension, their innermost reality. But he is present and acting there. Thus, all things are "from him," for he is the source of the reality of all things. All things are "through him" and "in him," for he is the ultimate support of their being and activity. All things are "to him," for he is the attractive impulse, drawing them into the future, building them up through the evolutionary process into more and more complex material arrangements and, corresponding to them, more and more intense centers of inwardness or consciousness. As God from within draws all things into the future, he unifies and orders them to make one universe. He draws our minds and wills to him in love, without compelling us.

The second thing to note is that by saying God acts in the within of things we are not excluding the influence of his power from the without. His power reaches all things, their within and their without, not as an external force interfering with the normal interaction of things, but from within as the ultimate interior unifying support and source of guidance.

God, then, is everywhere, in the within of everything, acting to maintain each thing in being, to guide its development and its relationship to other things and to himself. He inspires the love by which each thing tends toward the good suitable to it and to the universe.

This answer to the question "Where is your God?" is not of itself one calculated to inspire devotion and the life of prayer, for it says almost nothing about the personal quality of God's presence, about the attitude of love and intimate concern that he has, about the ultimate purpose he is working for: the sharing of his life and joy with those who are willing to be his friends. In particular, it says nothing about the Father and the Son coming to dwell in us in the gift of the Holy Spirit. However, it sets a context within which these matters can be recognized as genuine realities, not just imaginative metaphors. We will be exploring them throughout the rest of this work.

NOTES

1. John Courtney Murray, *The Problem of God* (New Haven: Yale University Press, 1964), p. 17.

2. Originally Psalms 42 and 43 were one psalm.

3. Similar prepositional expressions can be found in 1 Cor. 8.6, 11.12; Col. 1.16; Heb. 2.10.

4. See George Ernest Wright, *God Who Acts: Biblical Theology as Recital* (Chicago: H. Regnery, 1952).

5. Langdon Gilkey, *Religion and the Scientific Future* (New York: Harper and Row, 1970), p. 28.

6. "Many confusions in the doctrine of God and many apologetic weaknesses could be avoided if God were understood first of all as being-itself or as the ground of being." *Systematic Theology* (Chicago: University of Chicago Press, 1951), vol. I, p. 235.

7. John A. T. Robinson, *Honest to God* (Philadelphia: Westminster Press, 1963), chap. 3, pp. 45-63.

8. Ibid., p. 60. Emphasis in the original.

9. Gregory Baum, *Man Becoming: God in Secular Experience* (New York: Herder and Herder, 1970), p. 166.

10. Ibid., p. 58.

11. Gilkey, op. cit., p. 112.

12. See, e.g., John B. Cobb, Jr., *God and the World* (Philadelphia: Westminster Press, 1969).

13. For a somewhat more extended critique of process theology see my article, "The Method of Process Theology: An Evaluation," *Communio*, Spring 1979 (vol. VI, n. 1). With regard to Stoicism we may note that Stoic providence ruled the world in all its least details, determining exactly what happens at every step. The only freedom we have as human beings is to accept this willingly or be forced to endure it unwillingly. The identification of this view of God with what the Scriptures give was easily done and resulted in numerous controversies in Christian thought, e.g., the predestinationist controversies of the eighth and ninth centuries, Calvin's position on double predestination, the *de Auxiliis* controversies between Jesuits and Dominicans in the late sixteenth and early seventeenth centuries.

14. Cf. *Summa Theologica*, 1, 8, 1.

15. For a detailed development of Thomas's insight, see my article, "Divine Knowledge and Human Freedom: The God Who Dialogues," *Theological Studies*, Sept. 1977 (vol. 38, n. 3), p. 450.

16. Einstein, op. cit., p. 28.

17. Ibid.

18. Teilhard de Chardin, *The Phenomenon of Man*, 2nd ed. (New York: Harper and Row, 1965), p. 56. The whole of Book 1, chap. 2 is concerned with "The Within of Things," pp. 53-66.

19. Ibid., p. 55.

20. See Friederich Schleiermacher, *The Christian Faith*, 2 vols. (New York: Harper and Row, 1963), vol. 1, pp. 12-26.

21. *The Divine Milieu* (New York: Harper and Row, 1960), p. 48.

Chapter Four

Praise and Thanksgiving

The most characteristic and fundamental response to the presence and action of God in the world, as given in sacred Scripture, is the prayer of praise and thanksgiving. Theologically there are two principal questions concerning this prayer: 1) what is this kind of prayer? and 2) what difference does it make? There is a third question that grows out of the answers to these questions: do we praise and thank God for everything that happens, even painful and tragic events?

OLD TESTAMENT EXAMPLES
Psalms of Praise
Both the Old and New Testaments have many examples of praise and thanksgiving. Although only about one-sixth of the psalms are technically hymns or psalms of praise, still they so profoundly influence the spirit of the whole collection that in Hebrew the psalter is called simply *t^ehillim*, "praises."[1] The psalms of praise are characterized by two recurrent themes: the work of God in creation, in the glory and beauty of nature, and God's great deeds in history. Most of these psalms contain both themes, though some contain only one or the other, and all tend to emphasize just one of them. Psalm 33, for example, stresses God's work in creation, but indicates in general his involvement in history; it begins with an invitation to praise:

Rejoice in the LORD, O you righteous!
   Praise befits the upright.
Praise the LORD with the lyre,

make melody to him with the harp of ten strings!
Sing to him a new song,
  play skillfully on the strings, with loud shouts.
                                              (vv. 1-3)

A bit further on it introduces the theme of creation:

By the word of the LORD the heavens were made,
  and all their host by the breath of his mouth.
He gathered the waters of the sea as in a bottle;
  he put the deeps in storehouses.   (vv. 6-7)

His power over history and his protection of his people
is celebrated in the following lines:

The LORD brings the counsel of the nations to nought;
  he frustrates the plans of the peoples.
The counsel of the LORD stands for ever,
  the thoughts of his heart to all generations.
Blessed is the nation whose God is the LORD,
  the people he has chosen as his heritage! (vv. 10-12)

Psalms of Thanksgiving
Psalms of praise, then, acknowledge the power of God
at work in establishing and maintaining the universal
context in which human life is lived, the context of both
nature and history. Psalms of gratitude concentrate on
particular favors bestowed on an individual, or occa-
sionally on the community. Psalm 116, for example,
gives thanks for healing:

I love the LORD, because he has heard
  my voice and my supplications.
Because he inclined his ear to me,
  therefore I will call on him as long as I live.
The snares of death encompassed me;
  the pangs of Sheol laid hold on me;
  I suffered distress and anguish.
Then I called on the name of the LORD:
  "O LORD, I beseech thee, save my life!"

Gracious is the LORD, and righteous;
  our God is merciful.
The LORD preserves the simple;
  when I was brought low, he saved me.
Return, O my soul, to your rest;
  for the LORD has dealt bountifully with you. (vv. 1-7)

It concludes with the following promise:

I will offer to thee the sacrifice of thanksgiving
  and call on the name of the LORD.
I will pay my vows to the LORD
  in the presence of all his people,
in the courts of the house of the LORD,
  in your midst, O Jerusalem.
Praise the LORD!   (vv. 17-19)

Psalms of communal thanksgiving are rare, but Psalm
67 is one of them, in which the people give thanks for a
harvest. It ends in this way:

Let the people praise thee, O God;
  let all the peoples praise thee!
The earth has yielded its increase;
  God, our God has blessed us.
God has blessed us;
  let all the ends of the earth fear him!   (vv. 5-7)

The four themes which constitute the basic motives for
praise and thanksgiving turn out to be the traditional
areas of divine disclosure, the sources of our knowledge
of God: 1) God's action in creation, the world around us;
2) the great deeds of God in history; 3) personal experience, both in prayer and the rest of one's life as illuminated by prayer; and 4) communal experience, events,
or gatherings in which the people share together. For
the knowledge of God is always designed to lead to
praise and thanksgiving. This, in fact, is Paul's indict-
ment of the Gentiles: "So they are without excuse; for

although they knew God, they did not honor him as God or give thanks to him" (Rom. 1.20c-21a).

Glorifying God

Another Old Testament idea which captures these same insights into praise and thanksgiving is the divine glory. To praise and thank God is to glorify him. The divine glory is first of all the manifestation of the divine presence, as in the song of the seraphim in Isaiah's inaugural vision: "Holy, holy, holy is the Lord of hosts; the whole earth is full of his glory" (Is. 6.3). It is found frequently in the psalms as well: "The heavens are telling the glory of God; and the firmament proclaims his handiwork" (Ps. 19.1). God manifests his presence too, in his saving action: "Help us, O God of our salvation, for the glory of thy name; deliver us and forgive our sins, for thy name's sake!" (Ps. 79.9). But the divine glory is also our recognition and acknowledgment of this manifestation; this is to "give glory to God." Thus we read, "Ascribe to the LORD, O heavenly beings, ascribe to the LORD glory and strength. Ascribe to the LORD the glory of his name; worship the LORD in holy array" (Ps. 29.1). God's work in history is also reason to glorify him: "Sing to the LORD, bless his name; tell of his salvation from day to day. Declare his glory among the nations, his marvelous works among all the peoples!" (Ps. 96.2-3). The giving of glory to God is also a work of personal thanksgiving: "I give thanks to thee, O LORD, my God, with my whole heart, and I will glorify thy name for ever" (Ps. 86.12).

NEW TESTAMENT EXAMPLES
Fulfillment of Divine Promises

The writings of the New Testament pick up all these themes of praise and thanksgiving, but they stress the aspect of the fulfillment of divine promise in what God has done for us in Christ. The canticles of Mary, Zechariah, and Simeon to be found in the infancy Gospel of Luke all make this point (see Lk. 1.46-55; 68-79; 2.29-32). We may also note in particular the opening hymn of the Letter to the Ephesians, a rush of praise and thanksgiving that is only one sentence in Greek, strung together with relative pronouns, participles, and conjunctions. One has the impression that the writer is so overcome by the manifestation of divine mercy and grace in the mystery of Christ that he cannot bring himself even to stop for breath as he blesses and praises God (see Eph. 1.3-14).

In reply, then, to the first question posed at the beginning of this chapter, we may say that the prayer of praise and thanksgiving acknowledges God's goodness to us as shown in his works, in creation, in history, in our individual lives, and in the life of the community. We may even acknowledge and praise God's goodness in itself, the source and ground of all the gifts he bestows on us. The prayer that Jesus taught us begins as a prayer of praise: "Hallowed be thy name!"

PRAISE AND THANKSGIVING AS EFFECTIVE PRAYER
The second question about this kind of prayer is somewhat more difficult. What difference does it make? When I praise or thank a human person, it makes him feel good. Does God respond in the same way? What does the prayer of praise and thanksgiving do for us who offer it? Does it affect our relationship to God? Does it ready us for further gifts, as some have suggested? In trying to answer this second question, let us consider positively and negatively the consequences of praising and thanking God, and see what comes of doing it and of not doing it. All of this is to enquire whether and in what way praise and thanksgiving are effective prayer, i.e., do they as prayer produce some result, have some positive influence on the relationship between God and ourselves and one another, achieve some actual effect? And if so, how is this the case?

56

The Prayer of Faith
To understand the consequences of the prayer of praise
and thanksgiving it is important to recognize that this
prayer is precisely and essentially the *prayer of faith*, that
is, it is an acknowledgment of God's action in the world
together with an openness to receive that action into
oneself. It sees God at work in the world, in history, in
the life of the community, and in one's own experience;
it joyfully acknowledges this fact and accepts it into
one's life. Creeds as a rule are not the full, joyful,
human response to this action which belongs to the essential meaning of faith. Creeds thus express part of
what faith is about, but not its full meaning. Consider,
for example, the first article of the Apostles' Creed: "I
believe in God the Father Almighty, Creator of heaven
and earth " This acknowledges the basic activity of God
toward the universe: creation. Psalm 104 does the same
thing, but consider the difference in expression. It begins in this way:

Bless the LORD, O my soul!
O LORD my God, thou art very great!
Thou art clothed with honor and majesty,
    who coverest thyself with light as with a garment,
who hast stretched out the heavens like a tent,
    who hast laid the beams of thy chambers on the
        waters,
who makest the clouds thy chariot,
    who ridest on the wings of the wind,
who makes the winds thy messengers,
    fire and flame thy ministers.

Thou didst set the earth on its foundations,
    so that it should never be shaken.
Thou didst cover it with the deep as with a garment;
    the waters stood above the mountains.
At thy rebuke they fled;
    at the sound of thy thunder they took to flight.

The mountains rose, the valleys sank down
  to the place which thou didst appoint for them.
Thou didst set a bound which they should not pass,
  so that they might not again cover the earth. (vv. 1-9).

Effective Symbolic Activity

This then leads to the more fundamental question: what does the prayer of faith do? Stated most simply, *it brings to expression an essential dimension of our relationship with God*. This answer introduces us to a consideration which is of utmost importance for all kinds of prayers in whatever circumstances they are offered.

Between two human beings, to bring a relationship to some kind of conscious expression, to embody it in a symbol of some kind is the unique way to establish, sustain, strengthen, and deepen that relationship. Personal relationships really begin and grow only as they are expressed. Other things may provide a basis for personal relationships, like family ties; but these must be expressed somehow if they are to grow into genuinely personal bonds. Likewise, symbolizing and expressing in prayer the relationship between God and ourselves establishes, sustains, strengthens, and deepens that relationship. For the whole initiative of God toward us, all his gracious love and favor, all that he does in heaven and on earth is aimed at drawing us into a personal relationship with him, and only by acknowledging this action and expressing our acceptance of it can this relationship really be established and grow.

Thus Paul sees the basis of salvation in the expression of praise and faith, "Jesus is Lord." That this is an expression of praise is clear from the christological hymn of Philippians 2.6-11. Having recounted the incarnation, birth, sufferings, and death of Jesus, Paul refers to the action of God in exalting Jesus, giving him a name above every name (the name of "Lord") "that at the name of Jesus every knee should bow, in heaven and on earth and under the earth, and every tongue confess that Jesus Christ is Lord, to the glory of God the Father" (vv. 10-11). He tells us the consequence of this acknowledgment in Romans 10.9: "If you confess with your lips that Jesus is Lord and believe in your heart that God raised him from the dead, you will be saved." To praise God for his saving action in Christ is to open oneself to that very action, and hence to be saved.

The general principle can be expressed in this way: whenever we praise God for any action of his in nature or history or our own lives, we receive and deepen the effect of that action in us, and thus enter more completely into the relationship which God thereby initiates. Faith, expressed in praise and thanksgiving, lies at the heart of our entire relationship to God.

The Response from God
We may now answer directly the questions raised about the difference the prayer of praise and thanksgiving makes. Does it evoke a response from God? Everything that has been made known to us about God requires us to say yes. When we thank or praise another human person he is pleased because the relationship he intended in what he did or said or gave as a gift is being realized. God likewise rejoices in the realization of his will to share, his impulse to communicate his life and draw us into his friendship. Both the Old and the New Testaments use this kind of language. In Third Isaiah, as God speaks through the prophet concerning the final realization of His purpose in the New Jerusalem, we read: "For behold, I create new heavens and a new earth; and the former things shall not be remembered or come into mind. But be glad and rejoice for ever in that which I create; for behold, I create Jerusalem a rejoicing, and her people a joy. I will rejoice in Jerusalem and be glad in my people" (Is. 65.17-19). The New Testament frequently speaks of pleasing God, giving him joy by

acting according to his will (see Rom. 8.8; 1 Cor. 7.32; 1 Th. 2.4; Heb. 11.5-6). The parables of mercy in Luke 15 all end on a note of joy at the conversion of the sinner; the Good Shepherd rejoices to bring back the lost sheep; the woman rejoices to find her lost coin; the father rejoices at the return of his prodigal son. The accounts explicitly speak of joy "in heaven" and "before the angels of God" (Lk. 15.7, 10), expressions used often in Scripture to refer to God while preserving a sense of his transcendence. It is obvious, of course, that praise does not please God by way of "support" or making him feel important, as is sometimes the case with us.

Effect on Us
Do praise and gratitude do something for us who offer these prayers to God? Very much. They most significantly establish and strengthen the divinely initiated relationship. They deepen the presence of God's original gift to us, or at least intensify God's influence over us through his gift. Praise and thanksgiving always betoken acknowledgment and acceptance, ways in which we open ourselves to receive within us the effect of God's power.

Praising and thanking God in a group together binds believers to one another in their relationship to God. It makes them a people, God's people. For the action of God in nature and history seeks to establish a covenant relationship with all who will accept that action in faith. We manifest this acceptance in our common praise and thanksgiving.

Consequences of Ingratitude
What comes of not praising and thanking God? What are consequences of failing to respond in acknowledgment and gratitude?

At the least, when the neglect is a matter of oversight and ignorance rather than deliberate refusal, our personal relationship with God fails to grow as it might and could. It is not a question of God attaching some external punishment to the fact of our neglect; it is the neglect itself bringing about an inevitable impoverishment. God is more than willing to give the gift; but unless we receive it through praise and gratitude, the gift is not actually given.

At the worst, there are situations of willful blindness and proud refusals to acknowledge and be grateful. St. Paul describes the sinful situation of the Gentiles in these words: "Although they knew God they did not honor him as God or give thanks to him, but they became futile in their thinking and their senseless minds were darkened. Claiming to be wise, they became fools, and exchanged the glory of the immortal God for images resembling mortal man or birds or animals or reptiles" (Rom. 1.21-23). In this case the relationship to God is radically wrong; and this gradually poisons every other relationship through the dimension of selfishness manifested in the refusal to go beyond oneself. The influence of God's supporting and directing action, drawing us to one another and to himself in love, is suppressed as a person refuses to find a center and goal beyond himself and prefers to assert a false autonomy and independence. The consequences of all this Paul spells out in a terrifying passage, where he three times repeats the expression "God gave them up," meaning that God allowed the independence they asserted to bear its ultimate and poisonous fruit in their own lives (see Rom. 1.24-32).

THE PROBLEM OF EVIL
This brings us to a final question about praise and thanksgiving: Do we praise and thank God for everything that happens and affects us in some way? Do we, to be specific, thank God for natural disasters, for earthquake, famine, storm, and flood? Do we praise

him for disasters brought on by human agency, for war, oppression, slavery, and injustice? Do we thank God for our personal sufferings and disappointments? Certain views of divine providence would seem to say we should praise God for all this, for in some way he planned it. But unless such views are very carefully qualified they turn out to be more a position of Stoic philosophy than of Christian faith. It is far truer to say that we are not called on to praise and thank God for the painful and evil things that come upon us. However, we do praise God for his presence and power in this evil situation to draw good from it, to draw life even out of death.

The question we posed raises directly for a person of faith the single greatest problem and difficulty for complete trust in God: the problem of evil. Before sketching what seems to me the most adequate resolution of this problem, it is well for us to observe that the balance of things that happen is on the side of good; by and large, what happens is favorable to us, to our survival and development. Otherwise the human race would no longer be around.

Augustine's Solution
Traditionally, stemming largely from St. Augustine, there has been proposed a solution to the problem of evil that involves three steps:

1) Evil itself is nothing positive. It is a privation, the absence of something that should be present. Whatever is, to the extent that it is, is good. Evil enters only at that point where something ceases to be as it should be, ceases to have the fullness, order, or perfection that it should have. No being is evil in itself; something may be called evil because it lacks something it should have.

2) Evil enters the world with the abuse of created freedom. This privation or absence of good is that of disor-

der: the created will freely fails to direct itself to God as the supreme good. The possibility of such failure is inevitably linked with created freedom itself. God respects created freedom to such a degree that he does not prevent the disordered free choice from coming about; for he seeks the love and union of friends, not the slavery and bondage of robots.

3) All suffering, pain, anguish, and disappointment is traceable to some abuse of created freedom, not necessarily, however, to that of the one who is actually suffering. Sin lies at the root of all suffering; but my pain may reflect not my personal sinfulness, but rather my involvement in the sinfulness of the human race as a whole, what has been called "original sin."

In all of this, it must be added, God is at work to draw good out of evil. As St. Augustine explained: "Since God is supremely good, He would not permit evil of any kind in His works, if He were not so good and all-powerful as to bring about good even from evil."[2]

Another Perspective
The third point in this schematic answer to the problem of evil has seemed unsatisfactory to many. Even in the gospel, it must be remembered, when the apostles asked Jesus about a blind man, "Who sinned, this man or his parents, that he was born blind?" Jesus replied, "It was not that this man sinned, or his parents, but that the works of God might be made manifest in him" (Jn. 9.2-3). Jesus here seems to separate the evil and suffering of blindness from any connection with prior human fault. No doubt, much suffering would be eliminated from the world if we eliminated human sinfulness. War, racism, economic oppression, and environmental pollution are all linked to the abuse of human freedom. But it is the claim that this adequately explains *all* suffering and misfortune that meets with protests of dissatisfaction.

63

There is, however, a somewhat different approach to the problem of evil which allows the prayer of praise and gratitude to rise to God without reservation or reluctance. This approach stems largely from the thought of people like St. Irenaeus among the Fathers of the Church[3] and Teilhard de Chardin in recent times. It would agree that evil is to be thought of primarily in terms of privation and absence, but it makes three other points which are distinctive:

1) Some sin and suffering is statistically inevitable in this kind of universe, and the suffering doesn't all come from sin. Our modern understanding of the world as a universe in evolution and development helps us to see this. Evolution proceeds through a process of exploring many possibilities of adaptation and survival, and settling on those that actually work. It means that not everything is fixed and determined beforehand, even if a general direction and orientation can be seen in retrospect. This absence of predetermination is necessary, if the material world is to be an arena of freedom, a place where situations can be modified by the exercise of free choice. The world in evolution brings forth the human race whose members are called upon to respond freely in love to God and one another. But each person starts from a condition of immaturity, wrapped up entirely in concern for the satisfaction of his infantile needs, and is called upon to move to a condition of mature, unselfish love. That transition can hardly be effected without missteps, just as the unfolding of the material world in development cannot take place without defects, and without the replacement of one generation by another through the death of one and the birth of the other. It is no more possible for this kind of universe to exist without sin and suffering than a person could walk in the rain without getting wet. Perhaps some other kind of universe might exist without these intrinsic consequences; but it wouldn't be this world, and we wouldn't

be here to think about it. It isn't that God couldn't make such a world (we really don't know about this), but that he couldn't make *this* world without there being in it some sin and suffering, any more than he could make a square that didn't have four sides, or a living thing that didn't somehow respond to its surroundings.

2) It is good to have this kind of universe, in spite of the sin and suffering that goes along with it. It is not the sin and suffering that makes this a good kind of universe; it is rather the share in divine power and freedom which this kind of universe essentially embodies that makes us say with Genesis 1.31: "And God saw everything that he had made, and behold it was very good." There is a value to be found in a world whose members move through struggle and activity to a greater likeness to God, responding to the attraction of his goodness, and finally in freedom cooperating to establish a community of persons sharing truth and life and love with one another.

3) God acts to turn the inevitable sin and suffering to good. He does not merely regard the evil of the world from outside with affectionate concern and encouragement; rather, he enters into the world especially through the redemptive incarnation of his Son. He takes upon himself our sin and suffering. Our history becomes his history. From within he transforms this human condition marked by death, failure, and estrangement into one marked by the hope of everlasting life and communion with God. God does not plan all the particular sufferings that we experience; but he is present and active in every one of them to draw us through them to himself, to turn this evil into good. The great paradigm and supreme instance of the power of God to transform evil into good is the resurrection of Jesus Christ. The supreme act of human sinfulness was putting Jesus to death, an action that attempted deliberately to exclude from the world the unselfish love and

goodness of God embodied in his Son. All the wickedness of human history was concentrated in this act of rejection. But God was active in and through the love and obedience of Jesus, and the event of supreme human sinfulness defeating the plan and purpose of God became the event of our redemption, of freedom from sin, of God's victorious mercy. It is not of course possible to say in each instance how God draws good from evil, turns sorrow ultimately into joy. But the resurrection assures us that God is able to do this, if only we are willing. As St. Paul told the Roman Christians when they were threatened by persecution: "We know that in everything God works for good with those who love him, who are called according to his purpose" (Rom. 8.28).

We praise and thank God, then, not precisely *for* everything that happens but *in the face of* everything that happens. We can praise and thank him directly for what we recognize at once as good for us. But we can praise and thank him for his loving power which is at work to turn all things, even sin and suffering and death, to our ultimate well-being. Through this prayer we bring joy to the heart of God as his will to share his goodness achieves its purpose; and we deepen and intensify our personal union with him as we bring to expression our acceptance of his loving power in our lives.

NOTES

1. The main work of classifying types of psalms was done by H. Gunkel whose book was edited and published posthumously by J. Begrich: *Einleitung in die Psalmen* (Gottingen, 1933).

2. *Enchiridion*, chap. XI.

3. See John Hick, *Evil and the God of Love* (New York: Harper and Row, 1966), pp. 217-221.

Chapter Five

Prayer of Petition and Intercession

The problems of a theology of prayer are nowhere more acute than in dealing with the prayer of petition and intercession. It is easy enough to describe this kind of prayer. It is the prayer which corresponds most exactly with the radical meaning of the word "to pray," for it is asking God to do something or to give something. If the person praying is the one for whom the prayer is offered, it is the prayer of petition. If he prays for another, it is the prayer of intercession.

But what does this really mean? Are we trying to persuade God, to help him make up or change his mind? Are we, as some have suggested, just giving him the opportunity to do what he wanted to do anyway? Are we changing ourselves by praying so that we then become able to receive his gifts? (This might apply somehow to the prayer of petition; but how could it explain the prayer of intercession?) Are we, as some have set forth somewhat metaphysically, fulfilling the condition that he laid down ahead of time for the distribution of his gifts? And, most importantly, does anything ever happen that wouldn't have happened if we hadn't prayed? Finally, what does it mean to invoke the intercession of the saints?

These are just some of the more obvious problems connected with the prayer of petition and intercession. Before trying to answer them directly, let us consider briefly but carefully the teaching of Scripture. It seems at times that a secular attitude or a philosophical bias tends to write off the prayer of petition as wishful thinking. And if the person with this attitude or bias happens to be a theologian, the biblical data are usually entirely neglected or at least somewhat misrepresented. After considering the teaching of Scripture on the prayer of petition and intercession, we can try to gain a theological understanding of it suitable for men and women of the last quarter of the twentieth century.

In dealing with the biblical material on petition and intercession we will try both to get a clear idea of the attitude of the bible toward prayer of this kind and to discover the conditions required if such a prayer is to be effective. It is this matter of the conditions of effectiveness that especially concern us.

PETITION AND INTERCESSION IN THE PSALMS
Once again the basic Old Testament teaching is clearly and unambiguously set forth in the psalms. This teaching, simply stated, is that God hears prayers and answers them. Almost every kind of psalm, in more than fifty explicit declarations, proposes this as the truth about prayer. To appreciate the force of this teaching and to discover the conditions the psalms suppose for the effectiveness of this prayer, we will consider a number of these places.

Psalm 3, an individual lament or private prayer of petition, speaks confidently:

But thou, O LORD, art a shield about me,
    my glory, and the lifter of my head.
I cry aloud to the LORD,
    and he answers from his holy hill.   (vv. 3-4)

The "holy hill" is, of course, Mount Zion, where the temple is located. Thus, the one who prays does so as a member of God's people. This is confirmed by the last verse of the psalm:

Deliverance belongs to the LORD;
thy blessing be upon thy people. (v. 8)

Psalm 4, also an individual lament, expresses the ground of confidence in this way: "But know that the LORD has set apart the godly for himself; the LORD hears when I call to him" (v. 3). The Hebrew word for "godly" here is *chasid*; its root means "kind, pious," hence showing dutiful love to God.

In a prayer of thanksgiving, Psalm 9, attention is drawn to God's special care for those who seek him in trouble:

The LORD is a stronghold for the oppressed,
a stronghold in times of trouble.
And those who know thy name put their trust in thee,
for thou, O LORD hast not forsaken those who seek
thee.

Sing praises to the LORD, who dwells in Zion!
Tell among the peoples his deeds!
For he who avenges blood is mindful of them;
he does not forget the cry of the afflicted. (vv. 9-12)

The last line in particular shows God responsive to their prayer.

Royal psalms, which center on the anointed ruler of Israel, show God's particular concern for the king, who is charged with the welfare of the people. Psalm 18, for example, has the following lines:

I call upon the LORD, who is worthy to be praised,
and I am saved from my enemies. (v. 3)

In my distress I called upon the LORD;
to my God I cried for help.
From his temple he heard my voice,
and my cry to him reached his ears. (v. 6)

Great triumphs he gives to his king,
and shows steadfast love to his anointed,
to David and his descendants for ever. (v. 50)

Trust as an element of Old Testament prayer finds clear expression in the following passages from two individual laments:

In thee our fathers trusted;
　　they trusted, and thou didst deliver them.
To thee they cried, and were saved;
　　in thee they trusted, and were not disappointed.
　　　　　　　　　　　　　　　　　　　　　　(Ps. 22.4-5)

And:
Blessed be the LORD!
　　for he has heard the voice of my supplications.
The LORD is my strength and my shield;
　　in him my heart trusts;
so I am helped, and my heart exults,
　　and with song I give thanks to him.　　　(Ps. 28.6-7)

Wisdom psalms teach the value of turning to God in prayer, provided you endeavor to walk in his ways:

The eyes of the LORD are toward the righteous,
　　and his ears toward their cry.
The face of the LORD is against evildoers,
　　to cut off the remembrance of them from the earth.
When the righteous cry for help, the LORD hears,
　　and delivers them out of all their troubles.
The LORD is near to the brokenhearted,
　　and saves the crushed in spirit.　　　(Ps. 34.15-18)

Sincere worshipers likewise will find a hearing before God, as the following passage from a liturgical psalm shows:

Offer to God a sacrifice of thanksgiving,
　　and pay your vows to the Most High;
and call upon me in the day of trouble;
　　I will deliver you, and you shall glorify me.
　　　　　　　　　　　　　　　　　　　　　　(Ps. 50.14-15)

Finally, to conclude a list of examples that could be prolonged almost indefinitely, Psalm 86, an individual lament, summarizes in its opening lines much of what we have been considering:

Incline thy ear, O LORD, and answer me,
for I am poor and needy.
Preserve my life, for I am godly;
save thy servant who trusts in thee.
Thou art my God; be gracious to me, O LORD,
for to thee do I cry all the day.
Gladden the soul of thy servant,
for to thee, O LORD, do I lift up my soul.
For thou, O LORD, art good and forgiving,
abounding in steadfast love to all who call on thee.
Give ear, O LORD, to my prayer;
hearken to my cry of supplication.
In the day of trouble I call on thee,
for thou dost answer me.   (Ps. 86.1-7)

Conditions of Effective Prayer in the Psalms
As we try to gain some insight into the conditions which make the prayer of petition effective, some stand out with particular clarity. First of all, there are numerous references which recall the covenant and the promises which bind God and the psalmist together, references to "thy people," "his holy hill," "his temple," "our fathers," "his anointed," etc. But the mere fact of covenant is not enough; those who pray and are heard are described as "those who know thy name and put their trust in thee," "those who seek thee," "the afflicted," "the godly" (the kind and pious), "the righteous," "the brokenhearted," "the poor and needy," etc. We may add to these: "those who delight in the Lord" (Ps. 37.4), "those who know his name and cleave to him in love" (cf. Ps. 91.14), "those who fear thy name" (Ps. 61.5), and finally, "all who call on thee" (Ps. 86.5). What emerges from this is that the Old Testament strongly rejects any suggestion of magic. There is no hint that the human suppliant can through prayer manipulate God, produce automatic results, have God in his power. The

71

relationship between the one who prays and God is always personal, characterized by submission, love, praise, trust, and thanksgiving. Whatever sureness petitionary prayer has does not come from some kind of constraint exercised upon God; there are no automatic results that come from using appropriate words and gestures. The power of this kind of prayer lies in the quality of personal relationship that it expresses.

PETITION AND INTERCESSION IN THE NEW TESTAMENT
Gospels
The New Testament, in all the kinds of writings that make it up, likewise teaches that God hears and answers prayers. The Gospel according to Mark, after telling about Jesus cursing the barren fig tree, gives this teaching of Jesus: "Have faith in God. Truly I say to you, whoever says to this mountain, 'Be taken up and cast into the sea,' and does not doubt in his heart, but believes that what he says will come to pass, it will be done for him. Therefore I tell you, whatever you ask in prayer, believe that you receive it, and you will. And whenever you stand praying, forgive, if you have anything against any one; so that your Father also who is in heaven may forgive you your trespasses" (Mk. 11.22-25). In the Sermon on the Mount in Matthew we are warned about praying just to be seen: "And when you pray, you must not be like the hypocrites; for they love to stand and pray in the synagogues and at the street corners, that they may be seen by men. Truly, I say to you, they have their reward. But when you pray, go into your room and shut the door and pray to your Father who is in secret; and your Father who sees in secret will reward you" (Mt. 6.5-6). A little further on the following general teaching is proposed: "Ask, and it will be given you; seek, and you will find; knock, and it will be opened to you. For everyone who asks receives, and he who seeks finds, and to him who knocks it will be opened. Or what man of you, if his son asks him for a

72

loaf, will give him a stone? Or if he asks for a fish, will give him a serpent? If you then, who are evil, know how to give good gifts to your children, how much more will your Father who is in heaven give good things to those who ask him?" (Mt. 7.7-11). Another circumstance affecting the efficacy of prayer is given later in this gospel: "Again I say to you, if two of you agree on earth about anything they ask, it will be done for them by my Father in heaven. For where two or three are gathered in my name, there am I in the midst of them" (Mt. 18.19-20). Luke repeats many of these ideas (see, e.g., Lk. 11.1-13). He also provides an unusual parable on the power of persistent prayer, where God is likened to an unjust judge who finally yields to the importunities of a widow to vindicate her against her adversary. Jesus concludes this parable by saying, "Hear what the unrighteous judge says. And will not God vindicate his elect, who cry to him day and night? Will he delay long over them? I tell you, he will vindicate them speedily" (Lk. 18.1-8).

The Gospel according to John, in the words of Jesus at the Farewell Discourse, adds two other factors affecting the power of prayer: "Whatever you ask in my name, I will do it, that the Father may be glorified in the Son; if you ask anything in my name, I will do it" (Jn. 14.13-14). And: "If you abide in me, and my words abide in you, ask whatever you will, and it shall be done for you" (Jn. 15.7).

Acts and Epistles
The Acts of the Apostles gives many examples of prayers being heard: for restoration of life (9.40), liberation from prison (12.5-11), healing of disease (28.8). Paul's letters contain many prayers of petition and intercession. For example, he prays that he may succeed in visiting the Church in Rome (Rom. 1.10) and he exhorts the Philippians, "Have no anxiety about anything, but in everything by prayer and supplication with

73

thanksgiving let your requests be made known to God. And the peace of God, which passes all understanding, will keep your hearts and your minds in Christ Jesus" (Phil. 4.6-7). He also asks for prayers of intercession on his own behalf (see 2 Cor. 1.11) and of his prayers on behalf of others (see Col. 1.9-12). The remainder of the New Testament supports the same attitude toward the prayer of petition and intercession, as when the Letter of James stresses the power of prayer, especially the prayer of faith and the prayer of a righteous man (see Jas. 5.13-18). And finally the First Letter of John gives this general expression of confidence in the power of prayer: "And this is the confidence which we have in him that if we ask anything according to his will he hears us. And if we know that he hears us in whatever we ask, we know that we have obtained the requests made of him" (1 Jn. 5.14-15).

New Testament Conditions of Effective Prayer
Once again, the biblical view of the power of prayer as expressed in the New Testament has nothing to do with magic. The conditions of effective prayer are given as faith, which is the basis of all personal relationship with God, praying sincerely, praying together with others, praying reconciled with one another, praying in Jesus' name, abiding in him, praying with confidence, thanksgiving, and perseverance, praying according to God's will, praying as a righteous person.

To express the matter somewhat schematically, the New Testament teaching supposes that effective prayer of petition or intercession comes from one who is in personal contact and right relationship with God the Father, with Jesus, and with other human beings. This, however, means to pray in the Spirit, for it is the Holy Spirit who gives us this contact and relationship. The Holy Spirit is the gift of the Risen Lord to all those who believe in him (see Jn. 7.37-39; Acts 2.38). The Spirit enables us to call out "Abba! Father!" in addressing God

(Gal. 4.6; Rom. 8.15). He unites us to Jesus, as Paul makes clear in a passage in Romans: "But you are not in the flesh, you are in the Spirit, if the Spirit of God really dwells in you. Any one who does not have the Spirit of Christ does not belong to him. But if Christ is in you, although your bodies are dead because of sin, your spirits are alive because of righteousness" (Rom. 8.9-11). Notice the progression of ideas here: "the Spirit of God really dwells in you . . . [you] have the Spirit of Christ . . . Christ is in you . . ." And finally, the Spirit joins us to one another in the Body of Christ (see 1 Cor. 12.13; 2 Cor. 13.14; Eph. 4.3-4). And since it is the Holy Spirit who brings us into these relationships it is not surprising that we are encouraged to "pray in the Holy Spirit" (Jude 20), and that Paul teaches us that the Holy Spirit "helps us in our weakness; for we do not know how to pray as we ought" (Rom. 8.26-27). We ought further to observe that to pray in this way is to pray as a member of the New Covenant, the Covenant which makes us children of God, brothers and sisters of Jesus Christ, and brothers and sisters of one another in the gift of the Spirit.

THEOLOGICAL UNDERSTANDING OF PRAYER OF PETITION AND INTERCESSION
Three principles illuminate the meaning of the prayer of petition and intercession; two of them we have already considered. The first of these is that God is present and active in the within of all things. He is at the inmost heart of all reality, powerfully accomplishing his purposes. He is not present as a force alongside of other forces (this is activity in the without), but as *Alpha*, the ground and origin of the continuing reality of everything in the world, and as *Omega*, the attractive goal drawing all things from within into the future, continually building up the universe in a process of evolution and development which affects the without from the within, and continually drawing our minds and wills to

his love and thus building up the community of the human race in Christ and in the Spirit. God's power is not a dominating external force, but an all-embracing, unifying, upbuilding, internal, energizing source and attractive goal. His power does not interfere with or interrupt the interplay of external forces, but he uses and guides them, much as the human will uses and guides some of the forces within the human body.

Symbolic Expression
The second principle, dealt with first in connection with the prayer of praise and thanksgiving, maintains that bringing a relationship to symbolic expression establishes, sustains, deepens, and strengthens that relationship. We have considered that between human beings interpersonal relationships begin and grow only in and through some kind of mutual symbolic manifestation, a without that embodies and makes known a within. For example, friendship between two persons develops only as they express their attitudes toward each other in the exchange of words, smiles, gestures, gifts, etc. Between ourselves and God, the activity of praise and thanksgiving manifests our grateful acknowledgment and acceptance of his loving and powerful initiative toward us, in creation, history, community, and our personal lives. This manifestation of acknowledgment and acceptance allows the divine initiative to bring about the result God intends: an ever-deepening personal relationship with him and with one another.

The application of this principle to the prayer of petition and intercession is direct and centrally important. This kind of prayer also brings to expression, to symbolic manifestation, an aspect of personal relationship between ourselves and God and one another. The biblical data make this clear. Everything really depends upon the authenticity of this expression, on what is really being brought to manifestation, and hence is being established, sustained, deepened, and intensified. A formula of words, uttered either out loud or in the heart, may have the appearance of a prayer of petition or intercession. But it may actually be the expression of mere selfish concern, in no way growing out of or leading to a relationship of trust and love with God. In this event, it is not a prayer of faith, of openness to God and of acceptance of his power at work in the world, but an affirmation of self-centeredness, reflecting a desire to exercise personal domination and control. To pray, for example, to be freed from the need to care for my elderly parents because this interferes with my plans for a pleasant weekend at times, or to pray for someone's recovery of health because his illness is somehow an inconvenience to me, are both instances of "nonprayer" no matter how devoutly we may seem to be addressing God.

Expression of Faith and Trust
On the other hand, what we utter as a prayer of petition or intercession may be authentically a manifestation of faith and trust and a desire for deepening our relationship with God. What we ask for is sought within this relationship and contributing to it somehow. It is not, of course, necessary that this always provide the immediate and direct motivation; but behind our prayer, present implicitly and truly, is the desire to love God above all things and to love our neighbor as ourselves. If we pray for some kind of advancement, it is not to control others by our preference nor to profit by others' shortcomings, but ultimately to promote the kingdom of God and to be able to serve others in love. If we pray for health, it is not just for personal enjoyment nor to continue a way of life that is largely self-centered, but to make it possible for us to live and work for God. And there is always implicit in our prayer a recognition that even failure and suffering can be redemptive, and that death itself can mean a deepening of our relationship to

77

God in Jesus Christ our Lord. This kind of prayer is what John called prayer "according to his will," and such prayer is effective and does influence the outcome.

This principle also illuminates the prayer of intercession in a special way; for this prayer symbolizes our solidarity, our togetherness before God. What is given to each of us is to be shared in by all of us as far as this is possible. If our relationship to others is one of openness and caring and unselfish love, then our prayer of intercession brings to expression the order of dependence and communication that God intends in the world, and it is effective. But if our relationship to others is a matter of narrow, provincial concern, excluding some persons and finding some measure of our success in their failure, then our prayer of intercession does not express a desire for the coming of the kingdom of God, and it is not answered.

Divine Providence
The third principle, which has not been treated explicitly up until now, is the dialogical nature of divine providence. This is a conception of God's way of acting in the world as involving basically three moments: divine initiative, human response, divine response to human response. This conception provides the background for the understanding of the prayer of petition and intercession that is being proposed here. This conception of God's acting in the world, of interacting with the world, appears in the earliest traditions in the Bible that we can discover (the J document of the Pentateuch), and is constant from then on. We may briefly describe it in this way:

a) God out of pure liberality, in an act of absolute, gracious initiative, seeks to enrich us, by drawing us out of nothingness, and out of our littleness and poverty and self-centeredness and isolation, into a life of communion, sharing with him and with one another. This is divine grace.

b) The actual achievement of this divine purpose depends on our response to his free initiative. We must be willing to receive God's gifts in order to share them with others. We must be willing to renounce our self-centeredness, and to go out to God and to others, to abandon our fear and the supposed security of our own resources, and trust ourselves and our whole future to God's wisdom and strength and love.

c) Finally, God responds to our response to his initiative. This is the divine judgment in its most general conception, not just in the sense of condemnation. God effectively exercises his power according to our response. He gives us what we have opened ourselves to receive. But, in addition, because he loves us, he endeavors also to break down the resistance of our selfishness which opposes his desire to enrich us. This is what the Scriptures sometimes call the divine "anger." But it is an anger rooted in love, not vindictiveness.

Response to God's Initiative
Within the framework of this dialogical conception of providence, our prayer is itself a response to the divine initiative. God invites us to call upon him, draws us from within to seek from him what we need to live our lives in peace. When we pray we are responding to this invitation. Prayer is never trying to persuade a rich and powerful monarch to part with some of his wealth; it is taking our Father at his word when he tells us, "Call on me in the day of trouble, and I will answer you" (cf. Ps. 51.15). Our prayer of petition thus expresses our willing dependence on God as an essential element of our personal relationship with him which he initiates.

God's answer to prayer is his response to our response to his initiative. It is divine judgment, which most radically and positively is God's final redeeming and saving activity. God's answer to prayer is his expression in a concrete way of the realization of his purpose, the purpose which lies behind his invitation to call upon him, the purpose which inspires his gracious initiative in the first place.

God's Will
We may now try to answer some of the questions we raised at the beginning of this chapter. When we offer prayers of petition or intercession are we trying to persuade God, to help him make up his mind or to change his mind? Not really. We need to recognize that God's will to do us good sometimes remains in itself somewhat unspecified in the concrete. Just as he gives us the energy to act, but we freely decide in the concrete what precisely we are going to do, so also, his general intention to bless us and draw us to himself becomes specific and concrete in response to requests and prayers that are made "according to his will."

Are we through our prayers giving God the opportunity to do what he wanted to do anyway? The idea that prayer itself is a response to God's initiative indicates that this is to some extent the case. However, we should not conceive of God's intention prior to our prayer as so centered on one gift to be given that every other prayer or request must be disregarded.

Are we through prayer changing ourselves to make it possible for us to receive his gifts? Again, this is to some degree the case. But it does not mean that every instance of effective prayer of petition is a kind of conversion experience. It means rather that each time we pray we express and deepen our personal relationship to God. God's gifts to us, in whatever form they take, are further expressions of his loving care of us, in response to our desire to share more fully in his life. This is true also of the prayer of intercession; for our prayer for one another

80

strengthens the covenant bonds which make us brothers and sisters of one another and children of one Father. Our "togetherness" in mutual trust and forgiveness helps to constitute our situation of receiving and sharing the gifts of God.

Are we through our petitions and intercessions fulfilling conditions God laid down ahead of time for the distribution of his gifts? We can certainly say this, if we understand by it the general dialogical pattern of divine providence. What God does effectively in our lives is conditioned by our response to his loving initiative. Prayers of petition and intercession are simply special instances of these conditions. God's gifts are given in a developing relation of friendship only if we are willing to receive them as gifts; prayers of petition and intercession embody and make explicit this willingness.

Finally, does anything ever happen that wouldn't have happened if we had not prayed? Much, all the time. For if we genuinely pray, authentically manifest a personal relationship to God in faith, then our prayers as effective symbols enter into the order and instrumentality by which the whole of created reality is made present to God's ongoing and creative love. The world is being continually sustained and enriched as this love reaches it through the many complex interrelationships of actions, causes, and effective symbols. Authentic prayer is one of these symbols effectively relating the world to the enriching power of God.

THE INTERCESSION OF THE SAINTS
The intercession of the saints involves several points of theological reflection. First of all the general idea of the veneration or honoring of the saints grows out of biblical usage and prolongs it. A noteworthy summary of this biblical practice is found in Sirach 44–51, which begins, "Let us now praise famous men, and our fathers in their generations." This particular passage indeed lists only

men, but the Scriptures in general are concerned also about the great women of the Hebrew people and honor such persons as Miriam, the sister of Moses; Hannah, the mother of Samuel; Deborah, the prophetess and judge; Ruth, the ancestor of David; and Esther, the queen, recalled and honored at the feast of Purim. In the New Testament Hebrews 11 honors past heroes and heroines of faith.

Origin of Veneration of the Saints
The veneration of the saints first enters Christian piety in a notable and distinctive way as thanksgiving to God for the steadfast faith and love of the martyrs. The early Christians saw these men and women as embodying in themselves in a manifest and extraordinary way the power and grace and love of God, for in the face of threats, the loss of property, torments, and death itself they continued to confess Jesus as Lord and even to pray for their persecutors. Martyrdom was regarded both as an achievement of human fortitude and a supreme gift of God. Thus they spoke of the "palm of martyrdom," since a palm was the symbol of victory in a contest or struggle. Much of this is reflected in a passage of the Second Letter to Timothy: "For I am already on the point of being sacrificed; the time of my departure has come. I have fought the good fight, I have finished the race, I have kept the faith. Henceforth, there is laid up for me the crown of righteousness, which the Lord, the righteous judge, will award to me on that Day, and not only to me but also to all who have loved his appearing" (2 Tim. 4.6-8).

It became customary to recall the event of martyrdom for Christ each year on the anniversary of the martyr's death. The first centuries of the Church, up until the Edict of Milan in 313 gave legal status to Christianity in the Roman Empire, saw thousands of men and women of all ages, conditions, and ethnic groups within the

Empire remain faithful unto death in confessing the Lordship of Jesus. During these years, there were, of course, long stretches of peace, but a Christian had to be ready to die for the faith at any time, for they were continually regarded with suspicion. Thanksgiving to God for the lives and deaths of these people was a strong element of Christian piety and worship. The same praise of God was later extended gradually to include not only those who had died for the faith but also those who had lived it in an outstanding, exemplary way.

Communion of Saints
The second element which entered into the process leading up to the invocation of the saints was a sense of solidarity with those who had gone before, those who had fallen asleep in Christ, who were believed to be already sharing eternal life with Christ. The Letter to the Hebrews contains an expression of this sense of solidarity: "But you have come to Mount Zion, and to the city of the living God, the heavenly Jerusalem, and to innumerable angels in festal gathering, and to the assembly of the first-born who are enrolled in heaven, and to a judge who is God of all, and to *the spirits of just men made perfect*, and to Jesus, the mediator of a new covenant, and to the sprinkled blood that speaks more graciously than the blood of Abel" (Heb. 12.22-24). This sense of solidarity with deceased Christians now living with Christ was expressed also in the ancient baptismal creed as "the communion of saints."

This unity and community of all who believe in Christ is founded on his Lordship. As St. Paul writes to the Romans, "None of us lives to himself, and none of us dies to himself. If we live, we live to the Lord, and if we die, we die to the Lord; so then, whether we live or whether we die, we are the Lord's. For to this end Christ died and lived again, that he might be Lord of the dead and of the living" (Rom. 14.7-9). This sense of solidarity added an element of shared joy to the celebration of the anniversary of martyrdom. We rejoice with those whom we love and who continue to love us in their state of triumphant joy with Christ.

Mutual Love in This Communion
The third and final element of the process leading to the invocation of the saints grew directly from this sense of solidarity in faith and mutual love. If we show our love and appreciation for these saints by praising and thanking God for them and by rejoicing with them, how do they in turn manifest their love for us who are still struggling along the way? The spontaneous answer was that they pray for us as we pray for one another. Prayer of intercession among the living members of the Church is a firm practice from New Testament times. Thus Paul prays for the Thessalonians (see 1 Th. 5.23) and asks them to pray for him (see 2 Th. 3.1-2). He does the same in writing to the Romans (see Rom. 15.5-6, 30-33). The matter is well attested in other New Testament writings as well (see, e.g., Heb. 13.18-21; Acts 12.5, 12; Jas. 5.13-18). It was a simple matter to extend this to the saints who are already with Christ, sharing his glory. They pray for us as we pray for one another.

Communion in Sharing
This insight into the intercessory power of the saints highlights the essential structure of our communion with one another. "Communion" means sharing. We live in communion to the degree that what is given to each one is shared with the others. The gifts we receive remain always gifts, to be given to others as well. We speak of the "community of the Holy Spirit" (see 2 Cor. 13.14) because Christ shares his life with us in the giving of the Holy Spirit, and we are thereby enabled to share this life with one another, in rejoicing together, in bearing one another's burdens, in communicating faith and

confidence, and in many other ways, not the least of which is praying for one another.

Thus, to pray that God would grant us something through the intercession of some saint is to bring to expression our acknowledgment of this economy of divine giving. We are hereby recognizing that God gives to us not only directly and immediately himself, and not only through Jesus Christ and the Holy Spirit, but also (presupposing always those fundamental ways) through one another, both living on earth and living with Christ in eternal glory.

Christian piety has traditionally found two other expressions of this communion of all belonging to Christ: prayers on behalf of those who have died but are not yet glorified with him, and invocation of their intercession as they are being purified and prepared for the consummating vision of God. For although we know almost nothing about their condition, they are united in love with us and with God, and may thus intercede on our behalf even before their glorification, just as we do on earth for one another and for them.

VENERATION OF THE BLESSED VIRGIN
The special veneration of the Virgin Mary and the special trust in the power of her intercession grew out of the recognition of the special gift of God to her. For it was given to her, more than to any other human being, to enter through faith, humility, and steadfast love into the mystery of Christ. She was chosen to help constitute the mystery by bearing the Son of God and caring for his upbringing. She was also instrumental in the unfolding of this mystery by her presence at the foot of the cross, and by her prayer with the infant Church in the days before Pentecost. But the special gift that was given to Mary was given also to be shared, to be given to others. Thus, as we praise God for what he has done for her, and as we rejoice with her in her closeness to Jesus, her

Son, we also ask God to bless us through her. We pray that she would share with us the graces and blessings she has received from him.

No doubt it is possible to fall into exaggeration in the veneration of Mary and other saints. But this can happen only if we somehow separate them in our thinking and attitude from their dependence on God, his grace, the work of Jesus, and the gift of the Holy Spirit. To do this is to fall into a kind of idolatry. But if we keep the picture clear, with the power and love and grace of God at the center, then our prayers in honor of the saints honor God. Our love and praise of the saints reflects God's own attitude toward them. Our confidence in their intercession reflects our trust in the great love and graciousness of God.

Chapter Six

Growth in Prayer

Prayer brings to expression our relationship with God. But this relationship is not a static, formal reality given unchangeably once and for all; it is living and growing, developing and coming to maturity. It is an interpersonal relationship which grows as our response to God's initiative becomes purer, more enlightened, stronger, deeper, more intense. It is in these terms that we can speak about growth in prayer. And just as physical development is natural and inevitable apart from disease of some sort, so too spiritual development manifested in growth in prayer is also a normal phenomenon. Furthermore, prayer not only manifests growth in our relationship with God, it actively promotes and fosters this growth.

Spiritual Growth in the New Testament
The New Testament has many expressions relating to spiritual growth. The Gospel according to Luke tells us that Jesus' physical growth was accompanied by a development in the life of the spirit: "And Jesus increased in wisdom and in stature, and in favor with God and man" (Lk. 2.52). The parables of the kingdom of God frequently employ figures of growth and development. For example: "The kingdom of God is as if a man should scatter seed upon the ground, and should sleep and rise night and day, and the seed should sprout and grow, he knows not how" (Mk. 4.26-27). St. Paul is especially abundant in passages concerning growth. In the very first of his letters, the First to the Thessalonians, he encourages them: "Finally, brethren, we beseech and

87

exhort you in the Lord Jesus, that as you learned from us how you ought to live and to please God, just as you are doing, you do so more and more" (1 Th. 4.1). Faith and love are the aspects of Christian life about whose growth he most frequently expresses concern. He writes in 2 Thessalonians 1.3: "We are bound to give thanks to God always for you, brethren, as it is fitting because your faith is growing abundantly, and the love of every one of you for one another is increasing." He identifies God as the source of this increase in love: "May the Lord make you increase and abound in love to one another and to all men, as we do to you" (1 Th. 3.12). He distinguishes between the immature and the mature in Christ (see 1 Cor. 2.6; 3.1-2), a distinction found also in the First Letter of Peter when he writes: "Like newborn babes, long for the pure spiritual milk, that by it you may grow up to salvation; for you have tasted the kindness of the Lord" (1 Pet. 2.2). Finally, we may note a famous passage in Paul's Letter to the Ephesians which calls attention to both the individual and corporate dimensions of growth: "Speaking the truth in love, we are to grow up into him who is the head, into Christ, from whom the whole body, joined and knit together by every joint with which it is supplied, when each part is working properly, makes bodily growth and upbuilds itself in love" (Eph. 4.15-16).

Spiritual Growth and God's Presence
It is helpful to set this response of prayer and spiritual growth into the context of God's active presence in the world. We noted earlier (in Chapter 3) that God is present in the within of all things. He is there not as exercising external force and interfering with the normal interaction of things, but as the ultimate center within each thing. He is the source of their reality, the support of their being and activity, the impulse and attraction moving them into the future. God acts from within to unify and order all things. This presence of God is not

only personal but personalizing. Matter responds to this presence by an increasing complexity in the without and a parallel intensification in the within: the whole process of evolutionary growth and development. This response of matter is spontaneous and unreflective. But finally the human race appears each of whose members is called to be a free, conscious center able to respond freely and consciously to this presence of God. God calls each human being into existence through this evolutionary process, and he calls them each to respond in openness and love to himself and to one another for the establishment of an everlasting community of persons. Teilhard de Chardin has left us a description of this developing process:

"During immense periods in the course of evolution, the radial [the energy of the within], obscurely stirred up by the action of the *Primer Mover ahead* [God as Omega], was only able to express itself in diffuse aggregates, in animal consciousness. And at that stage, not being able, above them, to attach themselves to a support whose order of simplicity was greater than their own, the nuclei were hardly formed before they began to disaggregate [in death]. But as soon as, through reflection, a type of unity appeared no longer [merely] closed or even centered, but punctiform, the sublime physics of centers came into play. When they became centers, and therefore persons, the elements [individual human beings] could at last begin to react, directly as such, to the personalizing action of the Center of centers."[1]

This personalizing presence of God in the human within, in the depths of the human spirit, acquires a new and fuller meaning, as we shall see, with the gift of the Holy Spirit, who moves, unites, vivifies, illumines, guides, inspires, and pours love into our hearts. Growth in prayer means a growth in our personal response to this Center of centers, to God within.

Traditional spirituality has traced growth in prayer and the spiritual life through three stages: the purgative way, the illuminative way, and the unitive way. These were never conceived as three entirely separate stages through which one passed in such wise that nothing of the later was present in the earlier, and that as you went forward you left the earlier stage entirely behind. These are rather stages of emphasis, in which the activities of each stage are present in all stages, but not with the same centrality and concern.

The Purgative Way
In the first stage, the purgative, there is a special concentration on diminishing the force of responses that are alien to the attraction of God. These are the selfish, destructive, divisive, unloving responses which isolate us from one another and from God. What lies behind these responses, the movement of fear or anger or carnal desire, is radically and in itself necessary and good. But it is being manifested in a way that is self-centered and uncaring of others. Prayer at this time contains frequent petitions for forgiveness, for purification, for the single-minded desire to do the will of God, for strength and perseverance in good intentions. But it also contains grateful acknowledgment of God's unconditioned love bestowed on us without any merit on our part, the love that called us into being and now calls us to repentance and intimate friendship. Prayer in the purgative way is often accompanied by fasting or some other form of self-denial, which symbolically and effectively manifests the desire to turn from our selfishness to God.

The Illuminative Way
The illuminative way is characterized by heightened awareness. We become increasingly sensitive to the attractive power of God, to his presence within us, to his

life-giving love calling us beyond ourselves. The emphasis is on a kind of enlightenment, but it is much more a matter of knowing God personally in an I–Thou encounter than it is a matter of information or insight, though this too will be present to some degree. The prayer of the illuminative way is filled with praise and wonder, with thanksgiving and trust, with the desire to penetrate ever more deeply the divine mystery communicating itself to us. The persons at this stage will also become more aware of the presence and action of God in other people's lives. They will recognize the care and concern of God for the present social situation, see him in the poor, the neglected, the oppressed, and the disadvantaged, as well as in the gifted, the dedicated, the generous, and the unselfish. The illuminative way involves an intensification of faith and therefore a greater concern for justice.

The Unitive Way
The unitive way is especially the way of love. Our response to God's initiative becomes full and intense and unreserved and all-inclusive. St. John describes this union with God in terms of mutual indwelling as a result of love: "So we know and believe the love God has for us. God is love, and he who abides in love abides in God, and God abides in him" (1 Jn. 4.16). The prayer of a person in the unitive way is dominated by love, by self-giving, by joy in the divine presence, and by sorrow that God is too little loved. The love in the heart of a person at this stage is not directed simply and exclusively to God in Himself; as St. John also teaches us: "If we love one another, God abides in us and his love is perfected in us" (1 Jn. 4.12). Persons in the unitive way experience a three-fold oneness. They are one within themselves, in the harmony of their inner lives, in the integrity of their cognitive, affective, and ethical lives. They are one with God, Father, Son, and Holy Spirit.

And they are one with others in a community of love, forgiveness, acceptance, respect, and genuine care.

Anyone seriously intent on the spiritual life and the life of prayer will be aware of some characteristics of each of these three stages at all times. From the very beginning, in the midst of repentance, purification, and self-denial, there will be love and generosity. And even the mature person, walking habitually in the way of unselfish love, will discover something to be sorry for, some human failure to regret and repair. And throughout there will be light, growing realization, deeper awareness and sensitivity. Still, there is a normal progress of emphasis: from purification, through increased inner perception, to loving union.

HUMAN RESPONSE TO DIVINE INITIATIVE
To understand better this matter of growth in prayer it is important to recall that prayer is always human response to divine initiative. We can approach growth in prayer, then, both from the side of the divine initiative and from that of the human response. These are complementary aspects, the first of which we may call theological and the second phenomenological. The first considers the ways in which the divine initiative is perceived as more and more manifest and active in one's life. The second looks at the ways in which the human response normally progresses from lesser to greater fullness.

Trinitarian Initiative
It is in reflecting upon the divine initiative in the life of prayer that the meaning of the Trinity in Christian life becomes especially apparent. For this initiative of God drawing us into the divine life is not just an invitation issued from without, it is God entering into our lives, into our minds and hearts. And God enters by sending his Son, who dwells in our hearts through faith, and his

Holy Spirit, who pours his love into our hearts. The divine initiative in our lives is *mediated conceptually* to us through Christ; that is, as the symbol or sacrament of God, he reveals God to us, makes known to us the meaning of the Father's love. The divine initiative is *communicated powerfully* and immediately by the Holy Spirit, who is given to us as the Spirit of truth, unity, and love. These functions correspond in a way to the illuminative and unitive ways. Jesus, the Word, is described by John as the true light: "The true light that enlightens every man was coming into the world" (Jn. 1.9). As we accept him in faith, he gives us the Holy Spirit, the power to live as God's children: "But to all who received him, who believe in his name, he gave power to become children of God" (Jn. 1.12). This power is radically the Holy Spirit: "But you shall receive power when the Holy Spirit comes upon you" (Acts 1.8). (See also Lk. 24.49.) The Holy Spirit, as we have seen (pp. 74–75), unites us to the Father, to Christ, and to one another. The Son and the Spirit are always present together, reinforcing the influence of each other, and drawing us into the Father's life.

Jesus' Work
The work of Jesus in this regard is described for us in the Gospel according to John: "I am the way, and the truth, and the life; no one comes to the Father, but by me" (Jn. 14.6). The life, sufferings, death, and resurrection of Jesus Christ manifest to us visibly, unambiguously, and irrevocably the gracious, loving, saving initiative of God toward each one of us. For this reason, immediately following the words cited above Jesus adds: "If you had known me, you would have known my Father also; henceforth you know him and have seen him" (Jn. 14.7). When Philip, on hearing these words, says, "Lord, show us the Father and we shall be satisfied," Jesus replies, "He who has seen me has seen the Father" (see Jn. 14.8-9).

93

Contemplation of the Life of Christ

Hence, to understand God's loving initiative we need to contemplate or meditate upon the events that constitute the Christ mystery. This is not just an exercise of memory or imagination, a reconstruction through fantasy of Jesus' life. It means rather opening ourselves through faith to the ever-present action of God manifested to us in Christ. God's loving and powerful intention for us abides faithful and unchanging. What it is for us now is made known to us in the events of Christ's life. As we contemplate those events in faith God acts through them to transform us, to give us a share in Christ's life. As we turn toward him in love, he realizes in us, in all the events of our lives, his eternal purpose to make us his children. Paul writes: "We know that in everything God works for good with those who love him, who are called according to his purpose. For those whom he foreknew he also predestined to be conformed to the image of his Son, in order that he might be the first-born among many brothers and sisters" (Rom. 8.28-29). For this reason, the events of Christ's life, like the sacraments, are called "mysteries," since they too manifest to faith, in symbol and power, God's gracious, saving love.

Analytic Contemplation

There are two basic kinds of meditation or contemplation of Christ's life. We may term them the analytic and the synthetic. The analytic is the basic form and concentrates on single episodes or events in Christ's life. A person chooses some particular scene in the gospel and endeavors to discover in it the meaning of God's action and influence. Attention is directed especially to the interpersonal relations, manifested in what the people say and do. In any of these events, we can see that the interpersonal relationships of those who are involved with Christ are changed, developed, or modified in some way. It is here especially that the power of God at

94

work in Jesus is revealed, a power that continues to work in us and in our relations to one another. The personality of Jesus as transparent to the Father's love becomes for us a transforming power just as it was for the people who dealt with him at that time. The prayer suggested by St. Ignatius Loyola in the *Spiritual Exercises* is especially appropriate in making these meditations, the prayer for an interior knowledge of Christ, that I may love him more ardently, and follow him more closely. Growth in prayer and the spiritual life is above all growth in the knowledge, love, and following of Jesus.

Synthetic Contemplation
The synthetic form of contemplation grows organically out of the analytic. It is the normal and natural fruit of analytic meditation, for it gathers together a number of insights in a more unified way. Thus we begin to contemplate the courage of Jesus, or his honesty, his kindness, his mercy, or his strength; these are not just words with dictionary definitions somehow applied to him, but they are insights filled with concrete, living meaning derived from prayerful contemplation of actual events. Analytic and synthetic meditation are both concerned not only with "what" but with "who," but analysis concentrates more upon "what" as the avenue to the "who," while synthesis concentrates on "who" as the one who draws the various "whats" together into one personality. Synthetic contemplation therefore issues naturally into familiar conversation with Jesus, as with one known, admired, trusted, and beloved.

The mysteries of the life of Jesus and the facets of his personality illuminate the meaning of God's action in my life now. My response to God's initiative, my going to the Father through Jesus, is rooted in an appreciation of how he is present and active within me because of my openness in faith to what he has accomplished in and through Jesus.

But the initiative of God in our lives does not consist just in a formal content, the display of an ideal form of human life, prescriptions for religious excellence in imitation of Jesus. If that were the case, this initiative would be a new and heavier legalism. God's initiative is communicated to us immediately in the gift of the Holy Spirit as a power and energizing force. The New Testament continually points to the gift of the Holy Spirit as the distinctive mark of the Christian era, a gift given by the Risen Christ. Thus the Gospel according to Mark in its account of the initial preaching of John the Baptist has John make this distinction between Jesus' mission and his own: "I have baptized you with water; but he will baptize you with the Holy Spirit" (Mk. 1.8). The same distinction is repeated in Matthew 3.11, Luke 3.16, Acts 1.5 and 11.16. Peter's sermon on the day of Pentecost announces to the people: "This Jesus God raised up, and of that we all are witnesses. Being therefore exalted at the right hand of God, and having received from the Father the promise of the Holy Spirit, he has poured out this which you see and hear" (Acts 2.32-33). And in the Gospel according to John we read, "On the last day of the feast, the great day, Jesus stood up and proclaimed, 'If any one thirst, let him come to me and drink, as the scripture has said, "Out of his heart shall flow rivers of living water."' Now this he said about the Spirit, which those who believed in him were to receive; for as yet the Spirit had not been given, because Jesus was not yet glorified" (Jn. 7.37-39).

Illumination
It is not possible to detail here all that the Spirit accomplishes in the Church and in the lives of individual believers, but two aspects are important for growth in prayer. First, the Spirit is given to illuminate us, to recall to our minds the words of Jesus, to lead us into all truth, to bear witness to Jesus (see Jn. 14.25-26; 15.26-27;

16.12-15). This belongs to the mission of the Holy Spirit as the Spirit of Truth. The knowledge which is the Spirit's gift to us is not the communication of new information and ideas, but the realization and understanding, the appreciation of truth we have already learned and accepted. The Holy Spirit makes this truth "come alive" by establishing between us and it a kind of "connaturality." He gives us a taste and relish for this truth by inclining our minds and hearts toward it. This is especially what is meant by the gifts of wisdom and understanding.

God's Love Poured Forth
This illuminating function of the Holy Spirit is rooted in the other aspect of his mission which concerns us here. St. Paul tells us, "Hope does not disappoint, because the love of God has been poured forth in our hearts by the Holy Spirit, who has been given to us" (Rom. 5.5). Note that the locus of the Spirit's action is within, "in our hearts." The love of God spoken of here is not so much our love for God as God's love for us, following the Pauline usage elsewhere (see Rom. 8.39). The Spirit pouring forth God's love in our hearts gives us a positive and immediate experience of the reality of God's love for us, the creative, all-encompassing, unconditioned, freely bestowed, powerful, and saving love of the Father for us. For this reason St. Paul writes, "When we cry 'Abba! Father!' it is the Spirit himself bearing witness with our spirit that we are children of God" (Rom. 8.15-16).

It is the Spirit by this illumination and inspiration who leads us forward, thus manifesting the fact that we are God's children (see Rom. 8.14). The Spirit also enables us to acknowledge Jesus as Lord (see 1 Cor. 12.3). This is not merely an acknowledgment of Jesus' exaltation and power, it is also a recognition of his triumph as being for us, a triumph that began with his self-emptying in the incarnation, proceeded through his humility and obedience even unto death, and came to full expression in his resurrection and the confession of all creation that "Jesus Christ is Lord, to the glory of God the Father" (see Phil. 2.5-11). St. John finds the proof that God is love in the saving mission of Jesus Christ: "In this is love, not that we loved God but that he loved us and sent his Son to be the expiation for our sins" (1 Jn. 4.10). And he tells us that it is in the gift of the Spirit that the realization of this saving mission comes home to us: "By this we know that we abide in him and he in us, because he has given us of his own Spirit. And we have seen and testify that the Father has sent his Son as the Savior of the world" (1 Jn. 4.13-14).

Divine Initiative: Summary
The divine initiative, then, which is the fontal source of all growth in prayer and the spiritual life, is continually mediated to us through the events of Christ's life, and is communicated to us through the gift of the Holy Spirit. The life, death, and resurrection of Jesus teach us the meaning of growth; the presence and action of the Holy Spirit enable us to realize that meaning in our lives by a continually greater acceptance of God's initiative. We turn now to a consideration of this acceptance, our response to God's initiative, what we might call the psychology of prayer.

HUMAN RESPONSE
Freedom
In the context of growth in prayer, four observations about human response seem appropriate. The first is a caution not to try to program our response by deciding ahead of time how our prayer must grow and develop. Prayer and our relationship to God is the fruit of his free initiative toward us. Since it is free, we must leave room for him to surprise us, to lead us in new and unexpected

ways, to call us to himself in a way uniquely suited to our own personalities and the special friendship he offers us. Obviously, growth in friendship cannot be programmed, since it is the bond of freely bestowed mutual love. This means that we must let our prayer truly *be* response. Our way of praying must leave space for God to make his special light and attraction clear to us.

Growing Sensitivity
Still, we can point to certain general lines of development, to certain characteristics of growth which in one way or another are realized in a life of prayer faithfully and seriously pursued. And this is our second observation. Such a life manifests a continually greater sensitivity and concern to follow the initiative of God, the guidance of the Holy Spirit. Those who resist this growth in sensitivity become gradually insensitive. As we disregard the invitations of God through consciously accepting selfish motivations, our very awareness of these invitations diminishes. God, of course, can renew the power of his initiative in our lives in spite of our insensitivity, by leading us through sadness and desolation to recognize our need of him and our dependence upon him. In this way the whole process of deepening sensitivity can be renewed and reinvigorated.

Greater Mental Simplicity
Within prayer itself our mental activity tends to become more simple, less complicated. The beginning of a life of prayer is usually quite discursive, occupied with much reasoning, reflecting, questioning, comparing, forming convictions and attitudes. This is very important, but this activity becomes less varied and diffuse as the truth is grasped and relished in a simple look. It is now not so much a matter of discovery as it is of tranquil possession. In the contemplation of the life of Jesus analysis yields more and more to synthesis; the "what" leads more directly and deeply into the "who." Synthetic con-

templation is less and less gathering details into the unity of Jesus' living personality, and becomes more just being there with him, looking upon him with the serene gaze of faith.

Deepening Affectivity

As mental or knowing activity simplifies, affectivity grows and deepens. The emphasis shifts from thoughts, ideas, and convictions to responses of joy, awe, wonder, trust, gratitude, sorrow, love, and so on. These, too, tend to become more sustained and less varied, at least within a given period of prayer. As the human response, both on the level of knowing and willing becomes simpler and more focused, God may continue to draw the person through various kinds of purifications to a condition variously described as a brightness which is darkness to our minds, or a darkness which is brightness to the eyes of faith.

It is important to remember that none of this can be forced. If it is true that we must always be willing to move and to adapt, it is also true that our growth cannot go ahead of the divine invitation. Our prayer simplifies when it can no longer be complex, when multiplicity no longer nourishes us and only just being there is able to sustain our lives. It is well also to recognize that periods of transition often appear as "desert experiences." One way of praying, that for a long period perhaps offered strength and support, no longer works. A new way of praying has not yet developed. Having left one home we have not yet reached another. There is an enormous temptation just to give it all up, since nothing seems to be happening. It seems to us that prayer is not doing us any good, and there seem to be so many other important things to be done. It is here that great faithfulness and trust is necessary. Gradually things will clear, and, at least in retrospect, we will realize that God is with us through it all. Gradually, to us and to the world around us, the power of his love at work within us will

be made manifest through the transparency of our
humble acceptance.

Activity and Passivity
The third observation concerns the matter of activity
and passivity in prayer. It is frequently said that the
prayer of beginners is more active and that as time goes
on and prayer matures it becomes more passive. But it
seems to me that we must distinguish here our attitudes
and awareness from our actual activities and operations.
Initially, our attitude is more active than passive. We are
more conscious of doing and acting than of receiving.
We are more aware of what we do by way of response
than of what God does in his initiative. Gradually this
changes, so that we become more and more aware of his
action in us, illuminating, inspiring, strengthening en-
couraging, and so forth. This means, of course, that our
attitude becomes more passive. But our actual activity or
operation doesn't in itself become less. There is indeed
a greater dependence on God's action, and what we do
is done more freely, more simply, more intensely and
spontaneously. Our attention, then, is more upon God
than upon ourselves, but we are actually more active in
the real sense. For we see more clearly, believe more
deeply, love more purely, rejoice more unselfishly, and
so on. There is a kind of similarity here with a musician,
a pianist, for example. In the beginning such a one is
more conscious of his own activity, of discovering what
the notes mean, of trying to play the corresponding keys
on the piano, of correcting mistakes, of pedaling and
fingering and everything else that goes into interpreting
a piece expressively and faithfully to the composer's intent. But as time goes on, this all becomes second nature. The accomplished pianist is scarcely aware of his
own activity. His attention is all occupied with the
beauty of the music. And yet he is far more active than
the beginner. In both the case of the musician and the
one who prays there is a movement toward ecstasy, a

101

movement out of oneself into the other. But to see
ecstasy as simply passive is to overlook the intensity and
depth of the ecstatic response.

Vocal and Mental Prayer
The final observation concerns the distinction between
vocal and mental prayer. Is the latter to be considered
simply more advanced and more perfect than the other?
Does growth in prayer mean a gradual abandonment of
vocal prayer and an exclusive practice of mental prayer?
Not necessarily or normally.

The primary difference between vocal and mental
prayer is not found in the use or non-use of words.
Rather, in vocal prayer, the words are given to us, a
formula coming usually from the community, expressing
the fruit of the experience of many persons, like the
Lord's Prayer. Here the endeavor in prayer is actually to
mean what we are saying. In mental prayer no formula
is provided. We may or may not verbalize our response
to God's initiative. But here we must endeavor to say
what we mean, if we do indeed use words. We do not
try to impress God with our eloquent choice of words,
but to express as simply and as honestly as we can what
is in our hearts. The need for words may very well di-
minish over a period of time. Normally they tend to
become fewer both in actual number and in variety,
simply ways to focus the attention and the imagination
while "heart speaketh unto Heart."

Generally speaking, most persons have need of both
vocal and mental prayer. Prayer formulas whose senti-
ments are approved by centuries of use or by their own
inner obvious appropriateness serve as necessary re-
minders to us of responses we should make, of areas we
might overlook. They can enrich our prayer, especially
when fatigue or boredom lead us to forget what God is
doing for us or cause our own ability to express what is
in our hearts to dry up. On the other hand, these

102

ready-made formulas are not sufficient, since they cannot express the uniqueness of our own personality and circumstances. Nor do they provide us the space to listen to God, to discover those initiatives of his grace that are peculiar to the way he deals with us. For these reasons we need the greater freedom of expression that belongs to mental prayer. The excellence of one of these forms of prayer over the other is not to be judged from the presence or absence of a formula, but from the love and faith and humility that are brought to expression in the prayer.

GROWTH IN CONCERN FOR OTHERS

We may end this consideration of growth in prayer with an observation about the sociological implications of this kind of development. It might appear that drawing closer to God, to the transcendent Center of every life and of the whole universe, would mean drawing farther away from other persons, leaving the created world and its affairs behind. We would become so concerned about God that we become unconcerned about everything else.

But the exact opposite is true. Growth in prayer, if it is truly an increase in friendship and union with God, means growth in concern about other persons and what happens to them, for we come to share more profoundly God's care and concern for them. A development that isolates us from other people and makes us insensitive to their needs is a narcissistic illusion. Rather, as we come closer to the center of our own within, as we are joined in love to the God who dwells in our hearts, we are enabled to discover him as the Center within others, to rejoice and to praise him for the outpouring of his goodness in them. A good example of this is St. Paul. On the one hand he shows his concern for growing in union with God when he writes to the Philippians: "I press on toward the goal for the prize of the upward call of God in Christ Jesus" (Phil. 3.14). But this same letter is filled with expressions of his affection and concern for them; for example: "For God is my witness, how I yearn for you all with the affection of Christ Jesus" (Phil. 1.8). "Therefore, my brethren, whom I love and long for, my joy and crown, stand firm thus in the Lord, my beloved" (Phil. 4.1). These same two points could be shown from many other of his letters as well.

This then is growth in prayer, a life of words and deeds, of thoughts and affections, that effectively and authentically symbolize our deepening relationship with God and hence with others. This means sharing ever more fully in the life of God, the life that is mediated to us in the life, death, and resurrection of Jesus Christ, and is directly communicated to us in the gift of the Holy Spirit, the life that makes us members of the community of God, Father, Son, and Holy Spirit, and of all who are called to share this same life.

NOTES

1. *The Phenomenon of Man*, p. 271.

Chapter Seven

Friendship with Jesus Christ

God's gracious initiative in our lives, to which we respond in prayer, is mediated to us through the mystery of Christ. As we respond to this initiative there develops between the believing Christian and Jesus Christ a close personal relationship described in the New Testament in some detail. The thesis of this chapter is that this relationship may accurately be called "friendship" despite the many great differences between it and other human friendships. Establishing this thesis will involve examining the New Testament texts that describe our relationship to Christ, and making a simultaneous reflection upon the foundation and development of friendship as it exists between two human beings. From this will flow some important consequences for the life of the Christian community, for its apostolic endeavors, and for its efforts to achieve an appropriate visible expression of unity. We begin with a number of general observations, proceed to the more detailed consideration of the attitudes of the Christian toward Christ and their correspondence to the constitutive elements of human friendship, and conclude by noting the further implications of this relationship.

RELATIONSHIP TO CHRIST
A strong personal relationship to Christ is central to the meaning of our lives as Christians. The essential meaning of Christianity is not to be found in a new and superior form of ethics preached by Jesus, nor in advanced systems for promoting social welfare, nor even in human perfection conceived as my personal partici-

pation in divine life, but in a *koinonia*, a fellowship, a community, a network of interpersonal relationships between ourselves and God. At the heart of these personal relationships is relationship to Christ, a union made possible by grace, a union fostered and deepened through prayer. In the Farewell Discourse as given to us in the Gospel according to John, Jesus told his apostles, "No longer do I call you servants, for the servant does not know what his master is doing; but I have called you friends, for all that I have heard from my Father I have made known to you" (Jn. 15.15). Master and servant occupy two different worlds, isolated from each other. The concerns of the master, his activities and interests, his friends and associates are only dimly perceived by the servant. But Jesus assures his apostles, and through them us as well, that this is not the relationship he has with them. For just as the Father draws Jesus into the sphere of his life and concerns, so Jesus draws them into that sphere as well. We are called to be not simply servants of Christ, but his friends, sharing his friendship with the Father.

St. Paul summarized his relationship to Christ in a single concise expression: "For me to live is Christ" (Phil. 1.21). All that Paul does, all he hopes for, values, plans, dedicates himself to, counts on, seeks to accomplish, thinks, dreams about, all that living means to him is centered and brought to life in Christ. Paul's own detailed reflection on this relationship to Christ, which he sees as the call of every Christian, forms a major part of the evidence for establishing the thesis of this chapter.

We should realize from the start that friendship with Jesus is not a bit of sentimental day-dreaming. It is not like trying to be friends with George Washington or Julius Caesar, where no real personal communion is possible. Nor can we adequately describe this life of friendship by thinking in terms of good works that merit an increase of sanctifying grace. Not only is this too formal and abstract to be really helpful, it is too self-centered in its point of view. Nor are we to think that concern for developing friendship with Jesus Christ introduces us into a wholly undefinable world of mystical intuitions and experiences, a world where there are no guides, a forest without trails, a desert where we sit and wait for an inner inspiration of the Spirit, blowing we know not whence nor whither. It is possible, on the contrary, to say some very definite things about friendship with Christ, about growing in personal union with him. But we must first note that we cannot *make* him our friend; we cannot set down a series of rules, which if followed automatically constrain him to be our friend. You cannot make anyone a friend in this way.

Asking for and Accepting Christ's Friendship
But there are in general two things we can do: ask him for friendship, and accept his offer of friendship. Jesus assures us that if we ask our Father for the gift of his Holy Spirit he will not refuse us (see Lk. 11.13). Jesus manifests in his life and attitudes toward us this same unreserved love. He is in fact far more eager to come into our lives than we are to receive him. At the well-spring of all reality there is the eternal self-giving of God, which has become incarnate in Jesus Christ. This means that asking Jesus for the gift of his friendship is really part of the second general thing we can do: accept his offer of friendship. We are told in the Book of Revelation, "Behold I stand at the door and knock; if any one hears my voice and opens the door, I will come in to him and eat with him, and he with me" (Rev. 3.20). It is the Risen Lord, now living in the glory of the Father, who says this to us. The relation he invites us to share is life with him as he now lives. Our situation is very much like that of the disciples who met Jesus on the road to

Emmaus; when they pressed him to stay with them at
the inn, they were, without knowing it, accepting his
invitation to them to eat with him (see Lk. 24.28-29).

The more detailed description of our response to
Christ's invitation is fundamentally an analysis of what
our acceptance means. There are several basic attitudes
indicated in the New Testament. They can probably
occur in different orders and be expressed in different
ways. We will here consider six of them, which either
explicitly or implicitly enter into acceptance of friendship with Christ, and belong to growth in union with
him. The first of these is faith. It corresponds to getting
to know someone who is to be a friend.

FAITH

Faith in Christ is the total personal acceptance of Jesus
as real, as truly Christ and Lord, as Son of God and
Savior. It is not a decision to act *as if* I thought this were
the case, though it does issue in a commitment to live
according to what I have accepted. The New Testament
everywhere insists on the fundamental necessity of faith
in Jesus. The Synoptic Gospels portray Jesus as proclaiming the kingdom of God, and summoning his hearers to repentance and faith. But this faith extends in a
special way to the person of Jesus himself, not just to his
message and the kingdom. For example, he commends
the declaration of the centurion who said he was unworthy that Jesus should enter his home by replying,
"Truly, I say to you, not even in Israel have I found such
faith" (Mt. 8.10). To the woman who touched his gar-
ments in the hope of being healed of a hemorrhage,
Jesus said, "Take heart, daughter; your faith has made
you well" (Mt. 9.22). And to a blind man who called
after him, "Jesus, Son of David, have mercy on me!"
and asked to receive his sight, Jesus replied, "Go your
way; your faith has made you well" (Mk. 10.52). St.
Paul in explaining the crucial matter of justification
taught: "We know that a man is not justified by works of

the law but through faith in Jesus Christ" (Gal. 2.16). John, in the first ending of his gospel, gives Thomas's magnificent profession of faith, "My Lord and my God!" and adds two verses further on, "These things are written that you may believe that Jesus is the Christ, the Son of God, and that believing you may have life in his name" (Jn. 20.28, 31).

This attitude of faith lies at the heart of all friendship with Jesus because through it we are brought into living contact with him in his present reality. Paul prayed for the Ephesians: "that Christ may dwell in your hearts through faith" (Eph. 3.17). The Gospel according to John continually underlines faith as our opening to the saving power in Christ; he writes in the great statement of his theme: "For God so loved the world that he gave his only Son, that whoever believes in him should not perish but have eternal life" (Jn. 3.16).

Christ Cosmic and Personal
Jesus is not just a man who lived and died many centuries ago, leaving an indelible mark on history by his teaching and example. Right now he is alive, "seated at the right hand of God," which means that he shares with the Father divine rule over history. By his activity he now influences the course of events leading up to the climax of history at his Second Coming. He is the King of the universe, to whom the Father has subjected all things. St. Paul wrote to the Corinthians: "Then comes the end, when Christ delivers the kingdom to God the Father after destroying every rule and every authority and power. For he must reign until he has put all his enemies under his feet. The last enemy to be destroyed is death. 'For God has put all things in subjection under his feet'"(1 Cor. 15.24-27).

Christ exercises this cosmic mission, however, very differently from the remote, impersonal fashion of the executive of a large organization. He has, or seeks to have, an intimate personal relation with everyone for whom he died. He knows each of us in complete detail; no one is overlooked, blurred, or passed by. He tells us through the Gospel according to John, "I am the good shepherd; I know my own and my own know me, as the Father knows me and I know the Father; and I lay down my life for the sheep" (Jn. 10.14-15). Further, he loves us in the way he knows us, individually and personally; for the mode of loving always follows the mode of knowing. His attitude toward each of us continues to be what the Gospel according to Matthew said of him in his public life: "He will not break a bruised reed or quench a smoldering wick" (Mt. 12.20). He knows each of us just as we are, with all our faults, failings, discouragement, and sins, as well as our hopes, struggles, sufferings, and trust; and he loves us just as he knows us, just as we are. He does this, not because we have somehow earned this and are worthy of it, but because he is all good and seeks to bring our lives to fulfillment in him.

We accept all this by implication when we say in faith, "Jesus is Lord!" or, in the words of the creed, "I believe in Jesus Christ, God's only Son, our Lord." It is the first step in growing toward full friendship with Christ, just as the first step toward friendship with another person is getting to know him and to understand something of his interior attitudes, especially toward yourself.

REVERENCE

There is a second step which is taken almost as soon as the first, if acquaintance with another person is to lead to friendship. We may call this step esteem, respect, or admiration. It involves a more than ordinary appreciation of the other person's worth. Genuine friendship is more than just "liking someone," finding him pleasant company, easy to get along with. The company of a favorite dachshund might be this, but it is not friendship. This esteem grows as you come to know more about the other, and it leads to a desire for deeper

110

understanding, for a close relationship that may finally become friendship. It is clear, too, that this admiration, this appreciation of the other's personal worth, grows and remains as an integral part of true friendship. When "familiarity breeds contempt" it has not produced friendship.

Faith and Reverence
Likewise, faith in Jesus Christ leads almost at once to a profound sense of reverence. Indeed, calling him "Lord" is a mark of this reverence. We are advised in the First Letter of Peter to make this reverence a source of courage in the midst of those who inflict suffering upon us: "Have no fear of them, nor be troubled, but in your hearts reverence Christ as Lord" (1 Pet. 3.14-15). Our whole relationship with Christ must be penetrated by this spirit. There is no danger that this will make him remote and inaccessible; the real danger is that we might just get used to him, take him for granted, treat him as an equal, lose all sense of his unspeakable holiness, and hence cease to deal with the Christ who *is*, the real Christ. For those who are brought routinely into contact with Christ, through Scripture, sacraments, liturgy, and prayer in general, this is a very real danger. We can begin to assume the most casual of poses, showing not merely that we are "at home," but that we find nothing here out of the ordinary. Reverence, of course, is not just something external; it is essentially an internal attitude that will spontaneously manifest itself in some way—just as do all our other deeply felt inner attitudes.

Closeness to Christ
This union of reverence and closeness to Christ is clearly shown to us in the New Testament. The evangelist who identifies himself as "that disciple whom Jesus loved" (see Jn. 13.23; 19.26; 20.2; 21.7, 20) begins his gospel with the eternal Word through whom God made all things, and continues to describe the many ways in

which Jesus is one with God his Father. John the Baptist, whom Jesus described as the greatest man born of woman (see Mt. 11.11), spoke of Jesus, saying, "He who is coming after me is mightier than I, whose sandals I am not worthy to carry" (Mt. 3.11). St. Paul's most lyrical description of the unbreakable bond binding him to God's love in Christ is followed by an account of the great privileges of the Jews, the greatest of which is that from them, according to the flesh, comes Christ "who is God over all, blessed forever" (see Rom. 8.37-39; 9.4-5).[1] He also shows the close connection between knowing Christ and the sovereign appreciation of his worth when he writes to the Philippians: "Indeed I count everything as loss because of the surpassing worth of knowing Christ Jesus my Lord" (Phil. 3.8).

This attitude of reverence toward Christ is nourished by the New Testament description of our relationship to him and his function in the world. We depend wholly upon him: "There is . . . one Lord, Jesus Christ, through whom are all things and through whom we exist" (1 Cor. 8.6). "He reflects the glory of God and bears the very stamp of his nature, upholding the universe by his word of power" (Heb. 1.3). "Apart from me you can do nothing" (Jn. 15.5). He is the one from whom we will each one day hear the fateful word, "Come!" or "Depart!" (see Mt. 25.34, 41; 2 Cor. 5.10; Jn. 5.22). The New Testament reflects this attitude of adoring reverence in the doxologies or solemn prayers of praise directed to Jesus: "[May God work] in you that which is pleasing in his sight, through Jesus Christ, to whom be glory for ever and ever. Amen" (Heb. 13.21). "In everything may God be glorified through Jesus Christ. To him belong glory and dominion for ever and ever. Amen" (1 Pet. 4.11).[2] "But grow in the grace and knowledge of our Lord and Savior Jesus Christ. To him be the glory both now and in the day of eternity. Amen" (2 Pet. 3.18). "To him who sits upon the throne and to the Lamb be bless-

112

ing and honor and glory and might for ever and ever!" (Rev. 5.13).

This reverence for Jesus is not, however, just the attitude of adoration before him as the only Son of God; it is also a profound appreciation of his human qualities, his sincerity, strength, kindness, wisdom, compassion, and so on, qualities manifested especially in the way he deals with others. We nourish this attitude of appreciation by meditating on the mysteries of his life as given in the gospels.

It often happens that ennui or boredom in the spiritual life is dispelled by a renewal of the spirit of reverence and adoration. This helps us realize even on the level of our feelings the value, the worthwhileness of friendship with Jesus. The greatness of the one whose friendship we are privileged to enjoy generates a quiet enthusiasm and provides an abiding strength and support.

ABIDING SORROW FOR SIN

A third feature in the unfolding of human friendship may be called adjustment. As we come to know and respect a person, a desire for friendship will lead us naturally to avoid or correct what could reasonably offend him. We endeavor to adjust our way of acting to what will promote this developing relationship. It is not a question of pretending to be someone we are not, of disguising our real feelings and intentions, but of fostering what is best within us and relating to the other person with consideration and unselfishness. If we sincerely admire another person, it is no failure in sincerity to allow that admiration to affect the way we act, to let it lead us to change things about us that are objectively disagreeable.

What corresponds to this effort at adjustment in our relationship with Christ is abiding sorrow for sin. This is not a particular sorrow for specific failures; it is rather a

113

general acknowledgment of our sinfulness, an inner attitude of regret and a desire to repair the past and to improve in the future. For what obstructs friendship, what hinders our close approach to Christ, is not the sins we have committed themselves, but our continuing attachment to them. We can do nothing to alter the past fact of our failures; but that makes no difference, provided we do not remain voluntarily attached to them. Abiding sorrow for sin is precisely this attitude of detachment from sin, of rejecting what we formerly embraced. This is then to adjust our way of acting to the relationship we seek to have with Christ.

Reverence and Sorrow for Sin
The gospels show us how reverence for Christ leads to sorrow for sin in this general way. Early in his public life, Jesus asked Simon if he could use his boat to teach from, while the crowds listened on the shore. Afterwards he directed Simon to go out where the water was deep and let down his nets for a catch. In spite of the fact that he had worked all night and caught nothing, Simon obeyed, and his nets were filled to the point of breaking so that even his ship was sinking. Simon sensed the transcendent power at work. Acquaintance now led to reverence. He fell at Jesus' feet and exclaimed, "Depart from me, for I am a sinful man, O Lord." Here indeed was sorrow for sin. Jesus' response was not to depart from Simon, but to invite him to become a close disciple, a friend (see Lk. 5.1-11).

Zacchaeus is another example of one whose reverence for Christ led him to reform his life. Curiosity made him climb a sycamore tree to catch sight of Jesus. When Jesus called him to come down, saying He planned to stay with him, Zacchaeus came down joyfully and welcomed Him into his house. Then Zacchaeus, a chief tax collector, who had become wealthy by representing the pagan power of Rome in exacting tribute from his own people, said to Jesus, "Behold, Lord, the half of my goods I give to the poor; and if I have defrauded any one of anything, I restore it fourfold." Jesus' comment was, "Today salvation has come to this house, since he also is a son of Abraham. For the Son of man came to seek and to save the lost" (see Lk. 19.1-10).

St. Paul frequently expressed sorrow for his own past sinfulness, especially that of persecuting the Church before his conversion. "I am the least of the apostles, unfit to be called an apostle, because I persecuted the church of God" (1 Cor. 15.9; see also 2 Cor. 5.16; Gal. 1.13; Phil. 3.6-7; 1 Tim. 1.15).[3] Of the seven letters to the churches of Asia in Revelation 2–3, four contain exhortations to continued repentance for sinfulness (cf. Rev. 2.5, 16; 3.3, 19).

Genuine Repentance
Two extremes must be avoided in dealing with past sins. One is a depressing, anxious preoccupation with them, an attitude that is both self-regarding and implies doubts about the mercy of God and the reality of Christ as savior. It is a kind of "guilt complex." The other is an airy dismissal of the whole matter, a wish to forget all about it; things are now tidied up and the past never existed. We need to remember that of ourselves we are sinners, that if we are now as a matter of fact children of God, re-created by his grace, this is and continues to be the work of his transforming love. This spirit of repentance is a constant reminder of God's never failing, unconditioned love, and at the same time leads us to detachment from sin and to a life that is acceptable to him. Growing toward friendship with Christ will mean growth in the spirit of sorrow for sin.

GRATITUDE
The fourth attitude calls attention in a special way to the fact that friendship with Jesus is a unique and distinctive relationship for each one of us. It is gratitude. One can have many friends; but each one of them means some-

thing irreplaceably different. Friendship with many people is not simply the same identical relationship repeated again and again; in each case it is a new and fresh reality. The beginnings of a distinctive relationship to Christ are indicated in what has been said thus far, not so much in the matter of faith and reverence, as in abiding sorrow for sin, for each person's sins are distinctive historical occurrences. But the unique quality of each one's relationship to Jesus is especially underlined by the response of gratitude, for that for which each gives thanks is distinctively unique.

The usual language of the New Testament expresses gratitude and thanks to God the Father, as the one whose love and power lie at the root of the whole economy of salvation. But this is not done in an exclusive way, as if gratitude to Christ were negligible or unimportant. One of the deeply moving events of Christ's public life is the healing of the ten lepers. One of them, a Samaritan, perceiving that he was cleansed, returned "praising God with a loud voice; and he fell on his face at Jesus' feet, giving him thanks" (Lk. 17.15-16). How much this meant to Jesus is shown in the question he asked: "Were not ten cleansed? Where are the nine?" (v. 17). Jesus, however, regarded the thanks shown him as praise given to his Father: "Was no one found to return and give praise to God except this foreigner?" (v. 18). Paul is reported as thanking Christ for the ministry he has received: "I thank him who has given me strength for this, Christ Jesus, our Lord, because he judged me faithful by appointing me to his service" (1 Tim. 1.12). In the letter to the Colossians he sees thanksgiving as integral to life in Christ: "As therefore you received Christ Jesus the Lord, so live in him, rooted and built up in him and established in the faith, just as you were taught, abounding in thanksgiving" (Col. 2.6-7). The praise offered the Lamb in the Book of Revelation manifests a profound spirit of gratitude toward Christ:

116

"Worthy is the Lamb who was slain, to receive power and wealth and wisdom and might and honor and glory and blessing!" (Rev. 5.12). Very frequently thanks are offered to God through Christ, just as God's gift has come to us through Christ, e.g., "First I thank my God through Jesus Christ for all of you, because your faith is proclaimed in all the world" (Rom. 1.8).

But being grateful to God and to Christ seems to present a kind of psychological problem. We know we should be grateful. We say we are grateful and we sincerely try to mean this. But often we seem to experience or feel this gratitude only very feebly. Our feelings of gratitude toward someone who does us some trifling favor appear to be greater than those we have toward God. While it is true that feelings are not nearly as important as actually being grateful, this does raise the question of the quality of our being grateful to Christ, and whether we can improve this in some way. It seems to me that three things at least can be helpful.

Goodness of God's Gifts
First we should allow ourselves to experience the goodness of the gifts that God gives us through Jesus Christ. For this more than anything else, perhaps, it is necessary to slow up, and so be able to enjoy and appreciate this goodness. Rush, inattention, inner conflicts and anxieties can blind us to all we have received so that we take these things for granted and do not savor their worth: life, hope, friends, music, the earth, the stars— "Be still, and know that I am God" (Ps. 46.11). Be still, and let the goodness of what Christ gives come into your heart: faith, his grace and friendship, community with others, forgiveness, the Holy Spirit, the promise of eternal life, and the special gifts he gives to each one: "And his gifts were that some should be apostles, some prophets, some evangelists, some pastors and teachers,

for the equipment of the saints, for the work of ministry, for building up the body of Christ" (Eph. 4.11-12). St. Paul reminds us that we have nothing that we have not received as a gift (see 1 Cor. 4.7). From this he draws the consequence that we should not boast about what we have. It is also true that we should therefore be grateful for all we have. It is an invitation "to count our blessings"—but quietly, and in peace.

Christ's Personal Concern for Us
Secondly, we need to recall and experience the personal care and concern of Christ for each of us as manifested in these gifts. Impersonal beneficence rarely arouses gratitude. Who feels grateful to the post office for delivering mail? Or to the radio announcer for telling the time of day? It is not that we fail to value what they do; it is rather that we experience in this no special personal concern for ourselves and so are not stirred to personal gratitude. But all that Christ does is done for each one personally. St. Paul, in giving reasons why the "more enlightened" should avoid eating meat sacrificed to idols, admits that this practice is not wrong in itself. But some think it is and your example could lead them to violate their consciences. "And so by your knowledge this weak man is destroyed, this brother for whom Christ died" (1 Cor. 8.11). He speaks in the same way about the general matter of eating what some believe to be "unclean." "If your brother is being injured by what you eat, you are no longer walking in love. Do not let what you eat cause the ruin of one for whom Christ died" (Rom. 14.15). In both these cases Paul centers upon the individual Christian believer, for whom, he says, Christ died. Personal worth is in each case irreplaceably unique; Christ realizes and appreciates this. He cherishes each one, and his gifts are marks of this individual concern. St. Paul is urging us to have the same attitude toward one another.

118

Graciousness of Christ
Finally we should recall the utter graciousness of
Christ's gifts to us. We do not deserve them. We have
no claim upon him. We have, indeed, by our refusals to
allow his love to reign in us, made ourselves positively
unworthy of his gifts. But he has not therefore ceased to
love us. He continues to try to enrich us, and to make us
worthy of what he wishes to bestow. The thought of our
personal unworthiness should not depress or discour-
age us, for we recall it only in the context of our assurance that Christ unchangeably cares for us and is ready
and willing to heal us, if only we are willing to be
healed.

TRUST
Gratitude for the past leads spontaneously to trust for
the future, the fifth of this series of attitudes that add up
to friendship with Christ. It is clear once again from our
experience of purely human friendship that a friend is
someone upon whom you can rely. A relationship with
another person is always very close to real friendship
when you discover that you can count on this person to
be there when you need him, to offer help in whatever
way may be possible. The New Testament frequently
speaks of Christ as the unshakeable ground of our confidence. St. Paul triumphantly exclaims: "Who shall
separate us from the love of Christ? Shall tribulation, or
famine, or nakedness, or peril, or sword? . . . No, in all
these things we are more than conquerors through him
who loved us" (Rom. 8.35, 37). Christ's supporting love
makes him ready for anything: "I can do all things in
him who strengthens me" (Phil. 4.13). It is in the context of all that God has done for us in Christ that St.
Peter exhorts us, citing Ps. 55.22: "Cast all your anxieties on him for he cares about you" (1 Pet. 5.7). Jesus
in the gospel invites us, "Follow me!" (Mk. 8.34),[4] and
in this is asking for our complete trust; how complete he

indicates in his words to the apostles in the Last Discourse: "Let not your hearts be troubled; believe in God, believe also in me" (Jn. 14.1).

Christ, the Solution to Our Problems
In the profoundest and truest sense of the term, Christ our Lord *is* the solution to all our problems; he does not merely *have* the solution. He tells us, "I am the way, and the truth, and the life" (Jn. 14.6). "I am the light of the world; he who follows me will not walk in darkness, but will have the light of life" (Jn. 8.12). A problem arises in our life when something—a person, a place, a thing, an event, a temptation, anything at all—causes us anxiety and we can see no way out. If Jesus then comes into our life and has the place there that he wishes to have, that he should have, that he can have on the one condition that we are willing to accept him, then we no longer have a real problem. We may very well still have difficulties, sufferings, painful choices to make, even as he did, but we have no basic unrest or anxiety at the center of our lives, because Christ is there. This complete confidence in our Lord reaches every aspect and detail of our lives; not that each thing will turn out just as we might like it to, but that the final result, whatever it is, will be under the directing influence of his wisdom and power and love for us, personally. "I am sure that neither death, nor life, nor angels, nor principalities, nor things present, nor things to come, nor powers, nor height, nor depth, nor anything else in all creation, will be able to separate us from the love of God in Christ Jesus our Lord" (Rom. 8.38-39).

If we sum up the attitudes to Jesus we have considered thus far, we may express them simply in a prayer like this: "Jesus, my Lord, I believe in You. I worship and adore you as God's only Son. I am sorry for having offended you. I thank you for all I am and have and can be. I place my trust in you, for time and for eternity." Though all of this is indispensably necessary for friendship with Christ, it does not simply by itself equal friendship. Something further is required, something to which these attitudes themselves tend. Once again it is like purely human friendship. One may know another, admire him, avoid what he finds offensive, be grateful for various benefits, be confident that he will help when he can, and still not really regard him as a friend in the full meaning of that word. What is lacking in both cases is a special kind of love.

LOVE

It is clear from the New Testament that love for Jesus Christ belongs to the central meaning of being Christian. In the beautiful passage that opens the First Letter of Peter we read: "Without having seen him [Jesus Christ], you love him, though you do not now see him you believe in him and rejoice with unutterable and exalted joy" (1 Pet. 1.8). The dimensions of this love are indicated in the claim that Jesus makes in the Gospel according to Matthew: "He who loves father or mother more than me is not worthy of me; and he who loves son or daughter more than me is not worthy of me" (Mt. 10.37). St. Paul writes in the conclusion of his First Letter to the Corinthians: "If any one has no love for the Lord, let him be accursed. Our Lord, come! [Maranatha]" (1 Cor. 16.22). In the Second Letter he shows how central this is: "For the love of Christ controls us, because we are convinced that one has died for all; therefore, all have died" (2 Cor. 5.14). And the final verse of the Letter to the Ephesians reads: "Grace be with all who love our Lord Jesus Christ with love undying" (Eph. 6.24).

The Gospel according to John is the strongest in its expressions of the fundamental importance of loving Jesus. Love for Jesus manifests our relationship to God as Father. We cannot profess to be children of God and still fail to love Jesus. As he said to those who were opposing him: "If God were your Father, you would

121

love me, for I proceeded and came forth from God" (Jn. 8.42). Love of Jesus is the foundation for observing his commandments: "If you love me, you will keep my commandments" (Jn. 14.15). This then becomes the foundation for the Father's love and Jesus' self-manifestation: "He who loves me will be loved by my Father, and I will love him and manifest myself to him" (Jn. 14.23). This in turn is the basis for the divine indwelling: "If a man loves me, he will keep my word, and my Father will love him, and we will come to him and make our home with him" (Jn. 14.21). When the Risen Jesus confirms Peter in his position as shepherd of his flock, he asks him three times: "Simon, do you love me?" (Jn. 21.15-17). Thus, relationship to God as Father, observing the commandments, being loved by the Father, receiving the self-manifestation of Jesus, becoming a dwelling place for the Father and the Son, exercising pastoral office in the Church—all are linked to love for Jesus Christ.

Love of Desire
Thomas Aquinas observes that there are at least three ways in which we use the term love: love of desire, love of benevolence, and love of friendship.[5] In all cases there is a kind of affective inclination or attraction toward the person or thing loved, but the quality of the inclination is radically different in each case. Love of desire springs simply from the good that I can gain from the object of my love. I can love things in this way, like a delicious meal, which I have no intention of benefiting at all; quite the contrary. I can love persons in this way; I find them useful, pleasant, or amusing. In the last analysis it is more true to say that I love myself than the other when there is question merely of the love of desire. Love for Christ and the Father may begin this way, in the appreciation of them as the source of my eternal and true happiness. One may say that the damned con-

tinue to love God with a love of desire, and the frustration of this desire is the source of their greatest sorrow. Those afflicted with what we call spiritual pride may love God and Christ simply as the means to their own spiritual perfection.

Love of Benevolence
Love of desire looks to one's own good, but love of benevolence looks to the good of the other. To love another with the love of benevolence means to wish him well, to desire his good. When you give an alms or do someone a favor you are showing the love of benevolence. The person you love in this way may be someone you hardly know at all; he certainly need not be a friend in any profound sense. If a person were to serve God simply out of a sense of duty, he would have a love of benevolence for God, wishing him well, seeking to further his plans and his purpose. But there would be lacking any real personal involvement.

Love of Friendship
Love of friendship is more than mutual love of benevolence, though it manifestly includes this. Love of friendship is affective identification with another. "A friend is to a friend another self," St. Thomas observes, following many great writers of antiquity. One's affections, desires, purposes, and intentions are so taken up with the other person, the friend, that whatever touches or affects him by that very fact touches and affects you. You are deeply aware of the personal reality of your friend, his uniqueness and incommunicable, unrepeatable identity, and you regard that reality as your own, as another self. This love reaches out to another, not simply for what the other can give, nor just to enrich and benefit him, but in an attitude of personal identification with him. St. Paul wrote: "It is no longer I who live, but Christ who lives in me" (Gal. 2.20), and thus gave perfect expression to his friendship with Jesus.

This love of friendship for Christ has a sovereign quality, more than love of father and mother, son or daughter (see Mt. 10.37-39). It means making him the center of one's concerns, the spontaneous referent of all planning and hoping and desiring; no longer I but Christ. And this personal relationship is not just to "him" (in the third person), but to "you" (in the second). For we enter into an ongoing, developing intimacy in which he is always with us.

It is here that the paradoxical saying of Christ has its deepest application: "He who finds his life will lose it, and he who loses his life for my sake finds it" (Mt. 10.39). For to find one's life is to live with self as the center; and to do this is to live in an isolation from God and others that eventually means the loss of everything, including one's self. But to lose one's life for the sake of Christ is to live with him as the center; and this means to live in such an openness to God and all others that eventually you come into perfect communion with them, realize to the full the capacities of your life for love, truth, and friendship, and share "the joy of your Lord" (see Mt. 25.21). It is in this loving friendship with Jesus that we experience the saving loss of all things, including ourselves, and find ourselves enriched beyond anything we could imagine. Self-realization pursued as a primary goal is ultimately self-defeating; it is like trying to gain a good reputation by bribery or blackmail. But to pursue the realization of Christ in one's life through friendship with him, even though it may mean much renunciation of purely selfish concerns, results in a self-fulfillment that is all the greater for being his gift to us and not the fruit of our own unaided efforts.

Love, the Inclusive Response
This love for Christ includes and transforms all the other attitudes we considered earlier. As we put the living Christ at the center of our lives, love him freely and in

self-forgetfulness, accept finally and fully his invitation to friendship, we find that in a new and more vital way we believe in him, worship him, grieve for offending him, thank him, and trust him entirely. Love of Jesus Christ binds into the unity of friendship with him all the many attitudes we have toward him, and, indeed, forms an integral whole of all the activities, interests, plans, and concerns of our lives. Then the truest and most complete description of our persons is to say that we are friends of Christ.

CHRISTIAN COMMUNITY
It might at first seem that such an all-absorbing friendship would tend to exclude concern for anything else. Certain spiritual writings of an earlier generation likewise gave this impression. "Jesus-and-I" spirituality is taken as synonomous with a kind of supernatural narcissicism, a preoccupation with oneself and one's own private relationship with the Lord to the exclusion of everyone and everything else. Actually, if friendship with Jesus is genuine it leads to concern for the whole world. It does not isolate or divide, but unites and joins together at the profoundest level, where Christ is present to draw all to himself. Friendship with Christ lies at the heart of the love that we have for one another as Christians and which manifests itself in efforts to strengthen the Christian community and to draw others into this community through the preaching of the gospel. Friendship with Christ that fails to develop in this way is simply an illusion.

It is no doubt paradoxical that love for God and Christ is supposed to be total, unreserved, and unconditional, and that we are still supposed to love others genuinely, sincerely, and unselfishly. But this is the clear teaching of Christ and the apostles. When Jesus was asked about the greatest commandment of the law, he replied by giving the commandment from Deuteronomy; "Hear, O Israel: The Lord our God is one Lord; and you shall love the Lord your God with all your heart, and with all your soul, and with all your might" (Dt. 6.4-5; see also Mt. 22.37; Mk. 12.29-30; Lk. 10.27). But then, without being asked, he immediately states the second commandment, "You shall love your neighbor as yourself" (Mk. 12.31; see also Mt. 22.39). Love for neighbor is not something in addition to the love of God, a portion of love withheld from God that it may be conferred upon others. No: the very love of God in its total dedication to him embraces others as ourselves. When Jesus describes the Last Judgment, he makes it clear that our love and concern for those in need is love and concern for him, and our neglect of them is neglect of him (see Mt. 25.40, 45). In the Last Discourse, Jesus passes easily from his love for us, to our love for him, and our love for one another; these are all bound together indissolubly (see Jn. 15.12-17). That same close interrelationship is expressed in the First Letter of John (see 1 Jn. 3.14-16, 23-24; 4.9-11, 19-21).

Community with Christ and One Another
Two facts at least underlie this union among the followers of Christ. First, Christ loves each of us with a love of friendship and regards each of us as another self. Hence, to love Christ must mean to love those whom he loves, whom he regards as other selves, and to love them as he loves them. If we fail to do this, then our love for Christ is not yet the love of friendship but is arrested in its development somewhere on the level of the love of desire. Second, in loving Christ with a love of friendship we have each set him at the center of our lives. This unites us then in a common love of him and establishes a union among us that grows as we come to appreciate more the love that each of us has for him.

This understanding of community with Christ and one another gives an insight into one meaning of Christ's saving love. What is it that he finally saves us from? It is from the loneliness and isolation into which sin plunges us. The sinner retreats from the love of God into the love of himself. Then being centered only in himself he has lost all grounds for true communion with others. They appear to him as rivals and competitors, not as other selves. Sartre, in a famous line, stated: "Hell is other persons." For if this state of isolation is prolonged into eternity we call it hell, and this soul lost, since it is no longer able to reach its true destiny and home.

Christ saves us from this isolation of sin by extending to us his saving love of friendship. Those who accept this love begin to "live no longer for themselves but for him who for their sake died and was raised" (2 Cor. 5.15). As they accept "the eternal life which was with the Father and was made manifest to us" (1 Jn. 1.2), and enter into friendship with Christ, they have communion with other believers, "fellowship with us; and our fellowship is with the Father and with his Son Jesus Christ" (1 Jn. 1.3). This is the inner communion of the whole body of Christians, the invisible unity of the Church. It is rooted in loving friendship with Christ and with one another.

The visible divisions of the Church historically resulted not just from differences over doctrine, reform, or discipline, but also from a failure in love, on both sides of the division. We can observe the beginnings of the healing of these divisions as Christians of all kinds begin to regard one another with a love that has its roots in their common love of Jesus Christ. Those who love one another will find the solutions to questions of doctrinal belief, ethical standards, and Church polity. These problems are important, but they can remain divisive only if we fail to deal with one another in love.

APOSTOLIC WORK
Personal friendship with Christ likewise lies at the heart of the apostolate, the missionary effort of the Church. The effective proclamation of the gospel is like the spreading of a fire. Only one who is alive with the faith

127

and love of Christ can communicate that faith and love to another. The growth of the Church is not the outreach of a carefully organized bureaucracy, but the personal sharing of one person with another of what it means to know Jesus as Lord, Savior, and Friend. The institutional organization exists only to further this sharing; if it fails to do this or hinders it in some way, those responsible stand under the judgment of God. Whatever the legitimacy of their office, they themselves have become like the Pharisees of whom Jesus said, "Every plant which my heavenly Father has not planted will be rooted up. Let them alone; they are blind guides. And if a blind man leads a blind man, both will fall into a pit" (Mt. 15.13-14).

But those whose lives are centered in Christ, who love him with all their hearts simply because he deserves it, not because they are thereby made perfect and deserving of the respect of others, will want the whole world to love him in the same way, and they will work toward this end. And this is the apostolate.

All God's gifts to us are supposed to remain gifts, to be given to others. God's gifts enrich us as we share them with others. The more we share the more we are enriched. This sharing is the apostolate. But if we begin to regard these gifts rather as possessions to be hoarded than as goods to be shared with others, they will begin to evaporate. If we begin to center our lives in ourselves rather than in Christ and God, we will once again enter into the isolation of sin. There is no way in which the Christian life can flourish if it does not have a component of apostolic endeavor appropriate to one's place in life and the needs of the surrounding world, for the heart of apostolic endeavor is the love of Christ.

Finally, the gospels show us Christ as supremely conscious of a mission, a task given him by his Father, to proclaim and to inaugurate the kingdom of God. He calls on us to help him in this work. If our prayer has truly put us into contact with the living Christ, if we are truly his friends, we cannot be indifferent to his mission. As friendship means having him as the center of our lives, so it means working to realize his aims. And this is the apostolate.

CONCLUSION

Faith, reverence, sorrow for sin, gratitude, trust, and love—these are the attitudes the New Testament says we should have toward Jesus Christ. These attitudes constitute a relationship with him that can correctly be called friendship. From this friendship flows the living unity of the Christian community, and thus the effort to overcome our divisions and to proclaim the good news throughout the world. And all of this is begun and nourished in prayer.

NOTES

1. Some translators, relying more on what they think Paul should say than upon the Greek text, render this last clause contrary to the Pauline literary style everywhere else in his letters, "God who is over all be blessed for ever." Though they thereby eliminate Paul's extraordinary witness to Christ's divinity, the whole passage still conveys his profound reverence for Christ. For a discussion of the interpretation of Romans 9.5, see the corresponding note in *The Jerusalem Bible*, and Joseph A. Fitzmyer, S.J., "The Letter to the Romans," in *The Jerome Biblical Commentary* (Englewood Cliffs, N.J.: Prentice-Hall, 1968), n. 97, p. 319.

2. The Greek text makes it clear that the "him" of this passage is Jesus.

3. Although it may be questioned whether the last quotation is actually from Paul's hand, it represents an attitude consistent with Paul's other writings.

4. See also Mk. 2.14; 10.21; Mt. 8.22; Jn. 1.43; 8.12; 12.26; 21.19, 22.

5. Cf. *Summa Theologica*, 2a-2ae, q. 23, a. 1.

Chapter Eight

Discernment of Spirits

There are a cluster of phrases which describe, from somewhat different points of view, the ideal of the Christian life: "doing the will of God," "living a life of love," "following the guidance of the Holy Spirit," "imitating the example of Jesus," etc. Thus, the New Testament summarizes the life of Jesus as doing God's will: "When Christ came into the world, he said, 'Sacrifices and offerings thou hast not desired, but a body hast thou prepared for me; in burnt offerings and sin offerings thou hast taken no pleasure. Then I said, "Lo, I have come to do thy will, O God," as it is written of me in the roll of the book'" (Heb. 10.5-7). On one occasion, when his disciples pressed him to take food, he replied, "My food is to do the will of him who sent me, and to accomplish his work" (Jn. 4.34). The prayer of Jesus as he faced suffering and death gives the focus of his whole life: "My Father, if it be possible, let this cup pass from me; nevertheless, not as I will, but as thou wilt" (Mt. 26.39). The daily prayer of all Christians includes the petition, "Thy will be done on earth as it is in heaven." This is another way of expressing the kingdom or the reign of God, the fulfillment of his will. The will of God is not to be conceived as an impersonal piece of legislation. The will of God for us is essentially his love, so that doing the will of God means allowing God to love us effectively and allowing his love to flow through us in our love for others.

KNOWING GOD'S WILL

But before we can concretely choose to do the will of God, perform the deed of love, follow the light of the

Spirit, act in a Christ-like manner, we must *know* what this will is. No list of written commands or norms, however, is able to illuminate all the concrete situations of our lives sufficiently to make this known. St. Paul indicated this fundamental inadequacy when he wrote to the Corinthians, "The written code kills, but the Spirit gives life" (2 Cor. 3.6). The Christian life is a personal interchange between ourselves and God, like a conversation between friends. No set of rules or norms can tell you how a conversation ought to proceed, or what you ought to say next. A good conversation proceeds by a kind of instinct, each sensing the mood and attitude of the other, each responding in a way appropriate to that mood and attitude as well as to the subject being discussed. Thomas Aquinas observed that Paul's statement about the lethal quality of law applies even to the gospel if this is taken as a written code of conduct.[1] The New Law, he maintains, is the inner grace of the Holy Spirit.[2] An instinctive awareness of the Spirit's guidance constitutes the most immediate and concrete norm of our lives. It is not that the Spirit's guidance dispenses us from considering what written norms there are, and what their just requirements may be (see Rom. 8.4); it is rather that these are finally inadequate for telling us what to do. Life in a family, for instance, could never be reduced to a series of do's and don't's, although it is perfectly clear that some are necessary to set the framework within which the family may live together in support and understanding.

A Gift of God

Knowing the will of God is seen in the New Testament to be his gift, something to be sought in prayer, the fruit of dedication to him. One description of Paul's vocation, attributed to Ananias of Damascus, begins, "Brother Saul . . . the God of our fathers appointed you to know his will, to see the Just One, and to hear a voice from his mouth" (Acts 22.13, 14). Paul tells about his prayers for

131

the Colossians in these words, "And so, from the day we heard of it, we have not ceased to pray for you, asking that you may be filled with the knowledge of his will in all spiritual wisdom and understanding" (Col. 1.9). The reference to wisdom here is important; it appears again in the great hymn of praise at the beginning of the Letter to the Ephesians: "For he has made known to us in all wisdom and insight the mystery of his will, according to the purpose which he set forth in Christ" (Eph. 1.9). Later, in the same letter, he contrasts this knowledge with foolishness, which is the contrary of wisdom: "Do not be foolish, but understand what the will of the Lord is" (Eph. 5.15). The letter to the Romans uses the Greek word *dokimázein*, here translated "prove," to describe the knowledge of God's will: "Do not be conformed to this world but be transformed by the renewal of your mind, that you may prove what is the will of God, what is good and acceptable and perfect" (Rom. 12.2). This word has a connotation of knowing by experience, by testing and discernment. In context, it is seen to result from complete dedication to God; the previous verse reads: "I appeal to you therefore, brethren, by the mercies of God, to present your bodies as a living sacrifice, holy and acceptable to God, which is your spiritual worship" (Rom. 12.1).

Guidance of the Holy Spirit
Knowing the will of God means concretely being able to recognize the guidance of the Holy Spirit. The divine initiative is communicated to us immediately by the movement of the Spirit, as we noted in an earlier chapter, and we must learn to discern that movement from other motions and attractions. "For all who are led by the Spirit of God are children of God" (Rom. 8.14). At any moment we may experience many different inclinations and inspirations. We need to know which are from the Holy Spirit and indicate God's will to us, and which are opposed to God and lead away from him. In this

132

way our own personal friendship with Jesus Christ unfolds and develops.

It is well to recall that the God whose will we seek to know is not a distant, remote deity, but one who dwells within us as alpha and omega. He is there in a personal way, as the primal originative source of our whole being, inspiring and directing us into the future. He is there as the ultimate consummating goal, drawing and attracting us to himself. To choose according to God's will and to follow his Holy Spirit is to choose in harmony with this deepest impulse within us, the impulse that causes us to exist and moves us forward into what God's love plans for us.

THE PROBLEM OF DISCERNMENT
There are some situations of obvious moral decision where all the data are adequately subsumed under general norms: e.g., not killing the innocent, paying just debts. No circumstance is present to suggest that these general norms are here inapplicable. There is then no need to institute a process of discernment to discover God's will. Prayer may be necessary for the power to carry it out, but not to find out what it is. But there are two kinds of situations where discernment is necessary: first, where right or wrong is not the primary question, and second, where there appears to be a moral dilemma and every available choice seems somehow wrong.

The Permissible
The first kind of situation covers the whole area of the "permissible." No law or general norm either commands or forbids the choices which are available. After all relevant principles have been applied the matter is still unresolved. What should I choose for my life's work? Should I volunteer for this assignment? What person should I name to this position of responsibility? And yet, the choice may be very important. It may have long-lasting effects upon the whole course of my life

and upon my relationship with God. It is important to choose according to the will of God; this does not mean the will of God as it imposes an obligation, but the will of God as it lovingly invites me to receive from him the abundance of his life and to share that abundance with others.

Conflict of Rights
The second kind of situation presents conflicts of rights. No matter what I choose to do, someone is going to be hurt. There is no clear-cut, overriding priority that unmistakably resolves the tangle of obligations. Should I take this job which enables me to support my family, but makes it necessary to live in a place where my children's education will likely suffer? Should I go further into debt to keep my shop open, or should I fire half my staff who have been with me for many years? Should I continue working in this hospital to assist patients in grave need, or should I go out on strike to change unjust working conditions?

A Direction to Be Taken
In a situation where many choices are possible it does not seem necessary to suppose always that only one of these is according to God's will. When we pray to discover the impulse of the Spirit, we are not so much praying about a thing to be done as about an orientation to be followed, a direction to be taken. The will of God is dynamic, personal love urging me along the path that leads to him. As in making an ordinary journey, there may be several paths that lead to my destination equally well; or some way may be notably better; or some way may start out well but soon lead away from where I want to go; or there may in fact be only one way that really ensures arriving at my goal. The prayer to know God's will is a prayer to have this kind of insight about the choices open to me. Thus it may sometimes happen that I will actually be doing God's will, following the

guidance of the Holy Spirit, whether I choose this or that. But I must be ready also to receive the answer, "This alone is what I ask from you just now."

Another analogy suggests itself for focusing our problem. There are two opposed movements within the universe: entropy and evolution. Entropy is the loss of heat that takes place in every energy exchange. It means the diffusion of energy so that it is no longer available for any use. It is a winding down, a fragmentation, a drive toward corruption and death. Evolution, on the other hand, is an upward thrust, the elaboration of complex molecules, a process which unites, builds up, concentrates energy from the environment for use by the developing organisms. It is a drive toward union and life. As life can exist in many forms, with many varieties of beauty, so the movement of evolution can appear in many impulses. Entropy likewise can have many manifestations. The discernment of spirits seeks to distinguish similar movements in oneself: what is toward life and what is toward death? What is in effect evolution and development, what is entropy and decay?

This then is the problem whose solution is sought in prayer to know God's will. It is well to remember that the solution will not be found in some easy "rules of thumb." There is no automatic answer to such prayer. We never can manipulate God. But if we deal with him personally, from the center of our own freedom, in loving adoration and dependence, he will reply personally in continuing mercy and unfailing grace.

CONDITIONS FOR DISCERNMENT
The New Testament teaching on prayer to know the will of God lays down two conditions which are necessary for the effectiveness of this prayer. The two conditions are an attitude and an experience, which together consitute the "wisdom" St. Paul spoke of in dealing with the matter of knowing God's will.

Attitude of Unreserved Willingness
The attitude basically and most fundamentally is the
willingness to do the will of God whatever it may turn
out to be. It is important to observe that this attitude is
not just the fruit of our own good will; it too is a gift of
God, to be sought in prayer and received in gratitude.
This willingness is manifested in the sincere effort to do
God's will, to follow the guidance of his Holy Spirit,
where we do know it already. Where this effort is absent, this basic attitude is lacking. One who prays to
know God's will with a view to deciding afterwards
whether he will choose to do it, will never come to know
it, at least through the discernment of spirits. One who
prays without this willingness regards something besides God and the movement toward God as more important than God and his will; otherwise he wouldn't
have this hesitation.

We may observe this attitude in two places in the New
Testament. St. Paul has an extended passage on Christian wisdom in 1 Corinthians 2.6-16. He begins by speaking of a secret wisdom, a wisdom that is not of this
world nor of human origin. God has decreed this wisdom in his eternity for our glorification, that is, to lead
us to him (vv. 6-7). The rulers of this age showed their
complete ignorance of this wisdom by crucifying Jesus,
the Lord of glory, who was described earlier as the
power and the wisdom of God (v. 8; see 1.24). But this
wisdom, which is utterly beyond human experience and
human conception, God has prepared for those who
love him (i.e., for those prepared to do his will) and has
revealed through his Holy Spirit (vv. 9-10a). For the
divine Spirit alone knows what is most intimate in God,
just as the human spirit alone knows what is most intimate in a man or woman (vv. 10b-11). This Spirit, which
has no worldly origin but comes uniquely from God,
enables us to understand God's gifts to us (v. 12). Paul
imparts this kind of wisdom to the spiritual (v. 13; see v.
6), to those whose lives are led under the guidance and

impulse of the Spirit. But those whose lives are not under this guidance, who live only according to earthly wisdom following their own selfish impulses, simply cannot understand what Paul is talking about (v. 14). Paul concludes by saying that the spiritual man, one in possession of this wisdom, can judge all things, evaluate them from God's point of view. But no one can stand in judgment over him, since he knows the mind of the Lord, has the mind of Christ (vv. 15-16).

From this passage it is clear that one who is willing to follow the Spirit, who loves God and is prepared to do his will, who accepts the gift of the Spirit, is enabled to judge according to the mind of Christ. Such a one has the gift of wisdom simply hidden from those turned in upon themselves to live purely natural lives according to earthly norms. One who is so gifted is able to discover the will of God; the others are unable to recognize it at all. Later, in this same letter, Paul describes the ability to distinguish between spirits as a gift of the Holy Spirit (see 1 Cor. 12.10).

Another passage in the New Testament linking spiritual insight with the willingness to do God's will is found in the Gospel according to John. The occasion is the feast of tabernacles in what appears to be the second year of Jesus' public ministry. He is speaking in the temple, and his hearers marvel at his teaching, seeing that he has never studied. Jesus replies that he is not simply giving his own ideas (as his hearers might suspect in view of the fact that he never attended a rabbinical school), but the teaching of the one who sent him (see Jn. 7.16). How is anyone to know that this is so? "If any man's will is to do his [God's] will, he shall know whether the teaching is from God or whether I am speaking on my own authority" (Jn. 7.17). The willingness to do God's will confers such insight upon a person that he is able to judge about the divine origin of Jesus' teaching. The lack of this willingness brings spiritual blindness. As Jesus proclaims the will of God, his power to save and his universal love, those who are truly open to this will, perceive the truth of Jesus' words. The same condition for spiritual insight holds for us: we will be able to recognize the will of God only if we are willing to do it.

Experience of Peace and Joy
There is also a second condition required for the effective prayer to know God's will. It is closely related to the first condition, and is a special experience. To discover God's will through prayer one should have known at least once the peace and joy that comes from the complete gift of oneself to God, without any conscious reservation. This means that one has accepted the kingdom of God, his loving rule, into one's heart as fully and as completely as possible. Paul tells us, "The kingdom of God does not mean food and drink, but righteousness and peace and joy in the Holy Spirit" (Rom. 14.17). Paul first excludes a selfish way of life, preoccupation with food and drink, as constituting the kingdom of God. It is found rather in a right relationship with God, and in the experience of peace and joy that the Holy Spirit confers. Righteousness, this right relationship with God, comes from God as gift to those who have faith. Faith for Paul may be described as such a willingness to do God's will that one simply entrusts his whole life and destiny to him, accepting his word, relying on his promises. This kind of unreserved self-gift not only means the acceptance of justification or righteousness, but also leads to the experience of peace and joy which are unmistakable signs of God's kingdom, signs that no one else can duplicate or counterfeit. Paul's prayer for the Romans a bit further on confirms this understanding: "May the God of hope fill you with all joy and peace in believing, so that by the power of the Holy Spirit you may abound in hope" (Rom. 15.13). The peace which accompanies a life deeply rooted in Christ is also described by Paul in this way: "And the peace of God, which passes all

138

understanding, will keep your hearts and your minds in Christ Jesus" (Phil. 4.7).

This experience of peace and joy is certain evidence of the harmony between our own wills and the will of God in us. We may even be simultaneously experiencing suffering and pain; but deeper than all of this and freeing us from the anxiety and captivity it would otherwise induce, we know peace and joy at the inmost center of our awareness. We have as far as we are able simply and wholly put ourselves and all that concerns us in God's hands, and we experience the peace of his presence, the harmony of our wills with his will that sustains us in being and continually gives us all we have. The memory of this experience is a guide to recognizing where his will lies in other particular situations. Where we once again experience this kind of peace, even in small amounts, there we find the will of God, the harmony of our choice with his purposes. It can be distinguished then from every other kind of peace or inner satisfaction, which might come from some hidden selfish motivation. Without the earlier experience rooted in unreserved self-gift, it is possible to mistake some other joy for the peace and joy of God's rule within us.

NORMS FOR DISCERNMENT
The New Testament also gives us some norms to be applied to the possible choices that confront us, so as to discover thereby the will of God and the guidance of the Spirit. The most comprehensive norm comes to us from the teaching of Jesus. It constitutes a kind of major premise, one which needs to be supplemented by more particular considerations, which are like minor premises (to use the language of formal logic). The problem Jesus is dealing with directly is one that arose in the Old Testament: how do you tell a true prophet from a false one? It was explicitly discussed by Old Testament writers in at least two places; the solutions offered were not com-

139

pletely satisfactory, but they deserve consideration, at least to set the problem for us. One passage in the book of Deuteronomy, expressing the importance of the office of prophet in the life of Israel, directs that false prophets be put to death (see Dt. 18.20). Then it raises the question: "And if you say in your heart, 'How may we know the word which the Lord has not spoken?'—when a prophet speaks in the name of the Lord, if the word does not come to pass or come true, that is a word which the Lord has not spoken; the prophet has spoken it presumptuously, you need not be afraid of him" (Dt. 18.21-22).

The other passage comes from the story of the prophet Jeremiah. He had to contend with prophets who were reassuring the king and the city of Jerusalem that they had nothing to fear from the Babylonians. Jeremiah retorted: "The prophets who preceded you and me from ancient times prophesied war, famine, and pestilence against many countries and great kingdoms. As for the prophet who prophesies peace, when the word of that prophet comes to pass, then it will be known that the Lord has truly sent the prophet" (Jer. 28.8-9). Both these places, in slightly different ways, are directing us to tell a true prophet from a false one by seeing whether what they prophesy comes to pass or not. This criterion can be used only after the event, however, and is not too helpful in judging a prophecy about an event still to come. Jeremiah seems to add a further word in favor of the prophets of war, famine, and pestilence, but even that leaves something to be desired.

You Will Know Them by Their Fruits
Jesus deals with the problem in the Sermon on the Mount: "Beware of false prophets, who come to you in sheep's clothing but inwardly are ravenous wolves. You will know them by their fruits" (Mt. 7.15, 20). The last sentence provides the comprehensive norm. Jesus himself applies it in his confrontation with those who ac-

140

cused him of casting out devils by the power of Beelzebul (see Mt. 12.22-35). He first directly opposes the charge by showing its inner inconsistency, and levels a countercharge against his enemies, saying that they are uttering a blasphemy against the Holy Spirit, by attributing the manifest works of God to Satan (see vv. 22-32). Then, in v. 33, he reaffirms the principle of Matthew 7.20: "The tree is known by its fruit," and he applies it to his accusers: "You brood of vipers! how can you speak of good, when you are evil? For out of the abundance of the heart the mouth speaks" (v. 34).

Fruit of Faith and Mutual Love
This comprehensive norm can be applied to particular cases only by knowing what fruit to look for. If true and false prophets are to be known by their fruits, how can we recognize the difference between good and bad fruit? This is basically the same problem as distinguishing between spirits, as John reminds us: "Beloved, do not believe every spirit, but test the spirits to see whether they are of God; for many false prophets have gone out into the world" (1 Jn. 4.1). John himself in this context provides two particular norms: faith in Jesus, and love for one another: "And this is his commandment, that we should believe in the name of his Son Jesus Christ and love one another, just as he has commanded us. All who keep his commandments abide in him, and he in them. And by this we know that he abides in us, by the Spirit which he has given us. . . . By this you know the Spirit of God: every spirit which confesses that Jesus Christ has come in the flesh is of God, and every spirit which does not confess Jesus is not of God" (1 Jn. 3.23-24; 4.2-3).

However, it is St. Paul who gives us the most detailed description of the fruits which enable us to distinguish between spirits. Two passages are of the greatest importance: Galatians 5.16-26, where he describes the conflict between the Spirit and the flesh, and 1 Corin-

141

thians 13.4-7, where he lists the characteristics of love as opposed to selfishness.

Fruit of the Spirit

The conflict between the Spirit and the flesh is not a conflict between soul and body, but between the Spirit of God and human selfishness. This selfishness is symbolized by "flesh," meaning the perishable, weak, unredeemed aspects of human existence, as we live our lives cut off from God and rely upon our own resources. St. Paul has been insisting on the freedom from the law which Christ has given us, but he does not wish this freedom to become an occasion for licentiousness. This freedom is the power to live in accord with the deepest desire within us inspired by the Holy Spirit; it is not permission to do whatever we please in gratification of our selfish desires. He first affirms this basic conflict between Spirit and flesh (see Gal. 5.16-17), and then teaches that those led by the Spirit are not under the law, since, as he will explain, they are led and empowered to live in a way that is not contrary to the law (v. 17). He first enumerates the works of the flesh, the kind of fruit we bring forth when we follow the spirit of self-centered independence: "immorality, impurity, licentiousness, idolatry, sorcery, enmity, strife, jealousy, anger, selfishness, dissension, party spirit, envy, drunkenness, carousing, and the like" (vv. 19-21). He reminds his readers that those who live in this way will not inherit the kingdom of God. Then he lists the fruits of the Spirit—what we bring forth in our lives as we follow his guidance: "love, joy, peace, patience, kindness, goodness, faithfulness, gentleness, self-control"; and for those concerned about the law, he adds "against such there is no law" (vv. 22-23). St. Paul sees that this can come about only if we are willing to put to death our selfish desires: "And those who belong to Christ Jesus have crucified the flesh with its passions and desires" (v. 24). Hence, as we pray to know God's will we are

142

asking to see what animates a possible choice; where does it lead? If it tends to produce the sort of division and fragmentation and strife which are works of the flesh, it is not of God, no matter how well motivated we think we are. If, on the other hand, it leads to love, joy, peace and the rest, then we recognize the fruit of the Spirit and the choice he inspires.

Fruit of Love

Love is the first of the fruits of the Spirit; hence, when Paul tells us the characteristics of love, he is telling us the particular fruits we should look for as we try to discover the will of God and the guidance of his Spirit. (These characteristics are simultaneously a description of the personality of Jesus, which we are all called upon to reproduce in our lives.) "Love is patient and kind; love is not jealous or boastful; it is not arrogant or rude. Love does not insist on its own way; it is not irritable or resentful; it does not rejoice at wrong, but rejoices in the right. Love bears all things, believes all things, hopes all things, endures all things" (1 Cor. 13.4-7). St. Paul perhaps never wrote more famous lines than these, and they are a sure way to measure the degree to which love animates our lives and choices. They tell us unmistakably the fruit to look for as we pray to know how the Spirit is guiding us.

Before suggesting some ways in which God answers these prayers, we may briefly summarize this way of praying as follows: A person who wishes to discover God's will, when written norms are inadequate either because right and wrong are not the issue, or because a conflict of rights appears unresolvable, should approach prayer prepared to do whatever leads to God, whatever he wills. He should recall, at the same time, the memory of the peace and joy God has given at some time in the past. The prayer itself might take the form of these verses from Psalm 25: "Your ways, O LORD, make known to me, teach me your paths. Guide me in your truth and teach me, for you are God my savior, and for you I wait all the day" (vv. 4-5). This psalm adds a bit further on: "Who are they who fear the Lord? Them will he instruct in the way they should choose" (Ps. 25.12). As "the fear of the Lord is the beginning of wisdom" (Pr. 9.10), so those who fear God receive special divine guidance; for fear of God in the biblical sense implies a willingness to follow his will in everything, and usually includes the joyful experience of his great goodness.

TIMES OF DISCERNMENT

St. Ignatius in *The Spiritual Exercises* suggest three ways in which the answer to this prayer may come.[3] At times, God communicates an unmistakable conviction which it is impossible to doubt, accompanied by the peace and joy that only he can give. Though we cannot expect this kind of answer every time we pray, it is probably more common than many people think and is not confined to extraordinary events, like the conversion of St. Paul.[4]

The second way God answers this prayer is more gradual. We reflect upon the different impulses to action that we experience as we contemplate the different possibilities of choice. As we pray to know God's will and to be guided by his Spirit, we find that the peace and joy of God that we have experienced in the past are associated with some of these impulses and not with others. We continue this prayer and this reflection until it becomes clear to us which drives or impulses are in harmony with the presence of the Holy Spirit within us, and which are not.

The third way is somewhat more intellectual, but it is not strictly speaking a reasoning process. Here we do not consider just the drives and impulses, the attractions and repulsions, as in the second way, but we look also at the reasons or motives that occur to us for preferring each of the possible choices. We consider the *pros* and *cons* of each of them. It is not however just a question of weighing the reasons and so reaching a prudent decision; if this were possible, general norms and principles would suffice for making the right choice. Rather, we are led to recognize which reasons should be the decisive ones in this instance. Once again, it is the experience of the peace and joy of God as connected with certain reasons and not with others that enables us to recognize this. In all three ways, the actual choice should be confirmed by this same experience of peace. Here, of course, careful discernment is necessary to distinguish between a kind of relief at having reached some sort of decision at last (whether it is the right one or not), and that peace and joy which the Holy Spirit alone can give to us.

NOTES

1. *Summa Theologica*, 1a-2ae, q. 106, a. 2.

2. Ibid., a. 1.

3. Cf. op. cit., "Three occasions for making a sound and good election," nn. 175-188.

4. For a thorough discussion of this "time of election" and the other two as well, see Harvey Egan, S.J., *The Spiritual Exercises and the Ignatian Mystical Horizon* (St. Louis: The Institute of Jesuit Sources, 1976).

Chapter Nine

Liturgical Celebration

It is a simple matter to give a descriptive definition of
liturgical celebration. It is the public prayer and worship
of the Christian community visibly assembled together.
The purpose of this chapter is to discover what this
means, to offer some explanation of what is happening,
some insight into the underlying unity of divine and
human action that is brought to visible expression in the
event of liturgical worship. To achieve this we will reflect upon four matters: 1) the early development of
Christian worship as it is given in the Bible, 2) the liturgical symbolism of this worship, 3) the paschal mystery
of Jesus, which constitutes the heart of Christian worship, and 4) the diversity of gifts in the Christian assembly gathered for worship.

EARLY DEVELOPMENT OF CHRISTIAN WORSHIP
The service of Christian worship grew out of the Jewish
service and the tradition of worship in the Old Testament. This itself is an enormously rich and complex subject, but we may make a few observations pertinent to
our present consideration. Although all of the psalms
are, in a sense, liturgical, since they were used in the
temple worship, a number of them are designated
"liturgical psalms," since they depict or refer directly to
liturgical ceremonies. Among these we may note Psalm
24, which describes the entrance of a procession into the
sanctuary; Psalm 66, which depicts a ceremony of praise
and thanksgiving; Psalm 81, which gives a portion of
the liturgy for some festival, perhaps the feast of tabernacles; Psalm 95, which celebrates the divine kingship;

and Psalm 149, which invites worshipers to praise God by musical instruments and by dance. These help to convey the spirit of common joy and exultation that characterized much temple worship.

The book of Leviticus is a more practical liturgical book. Chapters 1 through 7 give descriptions of the various kinds of sacrifices to be offered in the temple. Chapters 8 through 10 contain the ceremonies for the consecration of priests to the service of God in the temple. The book goes on to give legislation on what is ritually clean and unclean, leading up to a description of the ritual for the Day of Atonement, Yom Kippur (chap. 16). There follows then the Holiness Code, which includes a list of the principal feasts of the year (chaps. 17–25). The book ends with some blessings and curses, and the way in which persons and animals vowed to the Lord could be redeemed (chaps. 26–27). The entire book makes clear the degree to which public worship was governed by various norms and directives.

Deuteronomy gives special insight into an aspect that was present at times in Hebrew worship: the renewal of the covenant, which set the entire context for the approach of the individual and the people as a whole to God. Thus in chapter 5, Moses is said to address the people in this way: "The Lord our God made a covenant with us in Horeb. Not with our fathers did the Lord make this covenant, but with us, who are all of us here alive this day" (Dt. 5.2-3). Later in the book, ceremonies of covenant renewal are expressly set forth (see 26.16-19 and 31.10-13).

Although the prophets frequently denounced a superficial worship and mere externality in community celebrations, several prophets, known as "cultic prophets," manifested special concern for worship, e.g., Ezechiel, Joel, and Malachi. Their special emphasis was on authentic, sincere worship.

From these brief references we may draw a few conclusions. The Israelite people came together publicly as the people of the Lord, assembled and called forth by him. They gathered to praise and thank him, to ask for his blessings and his forgiveness, and to renew the covenant which made them his people and him their God. Through priests they offered sacrifices, i.e., gifts which symbolized their self-giving and dedication to the service of the Lord their God. The liturgical celebrations themselves must be seen as events in the ongoing history of the people. They grew out of their past history; they brought to visible symbolic expression the present condition of the people before God; they directed them into the future, to live as his people and to await and work for the realization of his purposes. The continuing liturgy helped to make the history of this people.

Christian Worship
As the Christian community developed from being a special group within Judaism into a distinct group with its own structure, leaders, scriptures, faith, and common life of prayer, so too its worship developed gradually from the temple and synagogue worship into specifically Christian worship. A description of the earliest Christian community in Jerusalem has this: "And day by day, attending the temple together and breaking bread in their homes, they partook of food with glad and generous hearts, praising God and having favor with all the people" (Acts 2.46-47). The leaders of the Church in particular are described as taking part in Jewish worship: "Now Peter and John were going up to the temple at the hour of prayer, the ninth hour" (Acts 3.1). Peter and John got arrested on this occasion for healing a lame man and then proclaiming Jesus as Savior. When they were released the Christians together praised and thanked God for their release and prayed for the continuing success of the gospel (see Acts 4.23-31). Later on, in Antioch during a liturgical service

148

Paul and Barnabas received their vocation as apostles: "While they were worshipping the Lord and fasting, the Holy Spirit said, 'Set apart for me Barnabas and Saul for the work to which I have called them.' Then after fasting and praying they laid their hands on them and sent them off" (Acts 13.2-3). Toward the end of his missionary career Paul came to Troas for a week's stay. "On the first day of the week, when we were gathered together to break bread, Paul talked with them, intending to depart on the morrow; and he prolonged his speech until midnight" (Acts 20.7). (On this occasion, Paul's lengthy sermon caused a young man, Eutychus, to sink into a deep sleep and fall from a third-story window, killing himself. Paul was able to restore him to life. Many preachers in the history of the Church have achieved one of Paul's results.) We may note three things about this Christian assembly: it was on the first day of the week, Sunday, rather than the seventh day, the sabbath; it involved "breaking bread"; and it likewise involved preaching.

The expression "to break bread" used in this passage as well as in Acts 2.42, 46, became one of the very earliest designations of the celebration of the eucharist. The phrase occurs in the Old Testment only in Isaiah 58.7, Jeremiah 16.7, and Lamentations 4.4 where it refers to distributing food to the sorrowful, the poor or to hungry children; it was not a synonym for taking a meal together. In Palestine it was customary for the host to introduce the main course of a meal by breaking bread, a custom which Jesus followed when he fed the multitudes (see Mk. 6.41) and ate the Last Supper with his disciples (see Mk. 14.22 and parallels). It soon took on the meaning of introducing the Christians' commemorative meal (as in the account of Jesus eating with the disciples at Emmaus—Lk. 24.30, 35), and then came to designate the meal itself, which was the Holy Eucharist: "The bread which we break is it not a participation in the body of Christ?" (1 Cor. 10.16). Hence, when Acts speaks of Christians coming together to break bread, it is not referring to just any common meal taken together, but to the celebration of the eucharist. Breaking bread as an isolated gesture has no liturgical significance, but as introducing and designating the entire celebration of the Lord's Supper it refers to the heart of the Christian liturgy.[1]

As Christians began to receive Gentiles into their number, baptizing them into full membership and not requiring circumcision to make them Jews as well, a profound problem arose for the worship of the Christian community. Gentile Christians were not allowed to worship in the temple. Acts 21.27-29 tells how Paul was falsely accused of bringing Greeks into the temple and defiling the holy place. This led to his arrest, his long imprisonment and final transportation to Rome, though it was not for this crime alone that he was made to suffer. The exclusion of non-Jewish Christians from the temple worship meant that Christians had to develop more and more their own worship service. From the descriptions in Acts and from other New Testament writings we discover that this service contained four elements: 1) prayers, 2) readings, 3) preaching, and 4) celebration of the eucharist, though it is difficult to say in what order these occurred, or whether they were all present in each liturgical celebration. Unquestionably, there was a variety of celebrations from place to place and from one time to another.

Prayers included formal prayers, like the Lord's prayer, psalms from the Old Testament, and prayers offered "through Christ" to which the congregation responded "Amen" (see 2 Cor. 1.20). But there were also spontaneous prayers, including prayers in tongues (see 1 Cor. 14). And we should mention here the songs and spiritual canticles that were so often a part of Christian prayer together (see Acts 16.25).

Readings were drawn first of all from the Old Testament, since Christians were profoundly aware of the fulfillment of those writings in their own history. The Greek translation of the Old Testament, known as the Septuagint, became the primary scriptures of the Christian community, as this community became more and more Gentile and spread to include Hellenized Jews throughout the Roman Empire. In addition letters written to a particular church by an apostle were not only read in that church, but exchanged with others as well (see Col. 4.16; 2 Pet. 3.15). Accounts of the words and works of Jesus were probably first stylized in oral tradition and then written down to be read when Christians came together to celebrate the good news. Our four written gospels all bear marks of liturgical influences in their origin.

Preaching, teaching, prophecy, speaking in tongues and interpreting tongues, all were integral parts of the Christian worship service. Paul's accounts of the offices in the Church always make reference to these activities (see 1 Cor. 12.8, 10, 28-30; Rom. 12.6-8; Eph. 4.11-12). The word of God lived in the intercommunication within the Christian Church.

Finally, there was the celebration of the eucharist. Several expressions in Lucan writings suggest that in some places at least, this was a daily occurrence. As we noted above, "day by day" they broke bread together (see Acts 2.46). Luke's version of the Lord's Prayer does not ask for daily bread "today" as in Matthew 6.11, but "each day" (see Lk. 11.3). This eucharistic meal was not just sharing a meal together with Jesus, it was "proclaiming the Lord's death until he comes" (1 Cor. 11.26). Furthermore, it was a renewal of the covenant, of the new covenant in the blood of Jesus (see 1 Cor. 11.25).

These four elements have continued to constitute the basic pattern of Christian liturgy ever since the time of the apostles.

When the Christian community assembles to worship in this way, they symbolize through these four elements the deepest meaning of their reality as the People of God. For they manifest that they have been called together by God the Father as his children, redeemed by the blood of Jesus Christ, and led by the Holy Spirit; they manifest too their acceptance of the divine saving activity in their lives. As they symbolize this reality, they at the same time renew, deepen, strengthen, and prolong it. Once again, it is a matter of effective symbolizing, like all true symbolizing, but in a radically important way.

Reading the Word of God and preaching show this people as addressed by God, called forth and called together by his saving word to be his Church, his *ekklēsia* (Greek, meaning "those called out"). Reading and preaching, representing Scripture and Tradition, should not be sharply separated. For the preacher exercises his office not just by giving his own ideas, his own view of things, but by speaking from the abundance of a heart filled with faith, nourished by meditation on the Word of God in Scripture and the life of the Church. The preacher is called upon to articulate the guiding presence of the Holy Spirit today, in these circumstances. Hence, the Word of God here, too, addresses the people, just as Paul remarked about his own preaching to the Thessalonians: "When you received the word of God which you heard from us, you accepted it not as the word of men, but as what it really is, the word of God, which is at work in you believers" (1 Th. 2.13). Paul here stresses the ongoing power of the Word of God as it is received into believing hearts.

Prayer both precedes and follows the proclamation of the Word of God. As preceding, it manifests an attitude of attentive expectancy and a desire to purify the mind and heart of whatever could render them deaf and blind. As following, it manifests an acknowledgment of God's goodness and power, an acceptance in faith of what the Word has announced; it also asks for the continued presence and action of God in the days that lie ahead.

Thus, in these liturgical actions, we symbolize God's gracious initiative in the proclamation of the Word of God, and the human response of faith in the prayers and songs. It is through divine initiative and human response that we are constituted by God his people, the people of the New Covenant. It is true that God calls everyone to belong to his people, but only those who in one way or another accept this call in faith actually belong to that people. What word and prayer symbolize in this portion of the liturgy receives its fullest expression in the symbolism of the eucharist. For here is manifested the saving action of God in the paschal mystery of Jesus, and our response in faith, accepting, entering into, joining ourselves with this mystery. Thus, Liturgy of the Word and Liturgy of the Eucharist are profoundly one in their meaning, and together constitute but one act of worship. It is helpful to remember this in planning and celebrating the Christian liturgy.

THE PASCHAL MYSTERY
The paschal mystery in its fullness, which is brought to expression in the eucharist, is the movement of Christ from incarnation to glorification and the parousia. "I came forth from the Father and have come into the world; again, I am leaving the world and going to the Father" (Jn. 16.28). This movement of Christ is an effective action, in producing a New Creation; a sacrificial action, in worshiping the Father through total self-giving; and a community-building action, in forming a new people, reconciled to one another and to God.

The movement on the part of Jesus which constitutes the paschal mystery is not just taking a trip, going from

153

one place to another. It is an effective action, which in the first place transforms his own humanity from a condition of weakness, mortality, and suffering to one of power, glory, and eternal life. The movement of Jesus into consummation takes up into itself and brings to fulfillment the total evolutionary movement of the universe. This is the vision that inspired Teilhard de Chardin:

"Christ, principle of universal vitality because sprung up as man among men, put himself in the position (maintained ever since) to subdue under himself, to purify, to direct and superanimate the general ascent of consciousnesses into which he inserted himself. By a perennial act of communion and sublimation, he aggregates to himself the total psychism of the earth. And when he has gathered everything together and transformed everything, he will close in upon himself and his conquests, thereby rejoining, in a final gesture, the divine focus he has never left."[2]

It reflects a modern understanding of Paul's words to the Colossians: "He is before all things, and in him all things hold together. He is the head of the body, the church; he is the beginning, the first-born from the dead, that in everything he might be preeminent. For in him all the fullness of God was pleased to dwell, and through him to reconcile to himself all things, whether on earth or in the heavens, making peace by the blood of his cross" (Col. 1.17-20).

This movement is also a sacrificial action, for Jesus in this mystery of self-giving expresses his obedience and his worship of the Father. This has achieved matchless expression in the great christological hymn of Philippians 2.5-11, where the entire movement of Christ's life from incarnation to glory is recounted in terms of the self-emptying that found its ultimate expression in his obedient death upon the cross, and of the Father's act of accepting this offering and glorifying and exalting his

154

Son above the whole of creation. The Letter to the Ephesians directs us: "Walk in love, as Christ loved us and gave himself for us, a fragrant offering and sacrifice to God" (Eph. 5.2). All the New Testament references to the outpouring of the blood of Christ express the sacrificial quality of his dying and going to the Father.

A Community-Building Action
Finally, the movement of the paschal mystery is a community-building action, one that reconciles and unites the human race within itself and with God. The Gospel according to John gives this understanding of Jesus' death: "And I, when I am lifted up from the earth, will draw all men to myself" (Jn. 12.32). And in the prayer of Jesus at the Last Supper his sacrificial act of "consecrating" himself is immediately joined to the desire for unity among his followers: "And for their sake I consecrate myself, that they also may be consecrated in truth. I do not pray for these only but also for those who are to believe in me through their word, that they may all be one; even as thou, Father, art in me, and I in thee, that they also may be in us, so that the world may believe that thou hast sent me" (Jn. 17.19-21). The reconciling power of the death of Jesus on the cross is a central message in the Letter to the Ephesians: "For he is our peace, who has made us both one, and has broken down the dividing wall of hostility, by abolishing in his flesh the law of commandments and ordinances, that he might create in himself one new man in place of the two, so making peace, and might reconcile us both to God in one body through the cross, thereby bringing the hostility to an end" (Eph. 2.14-16). This movement now makes real the community of believers, the Church, through the continual gift of the Holy Spirit from the Risen Christ. He is called by St. Paul "the last Adam" because as a life-giving Spirit he constitutes believers as a new race in himself (see 1 Cor. 15.45). The movement reaches its full completion in the parousia: "Then comes

155

the end, when he delivers the kingdom to God the Father after destroying every rule and every authority and power. For he must reign until he has put all his enemies under his feet" (1 Cor. 15.24-25). This is the final realization of the plan of God described in Ephesians: "In him we have redemption through his blood, the forgiveness of our trespasses, according to the riches of his grace which he lavished upon us. For he has made known to us in all wisdom and insight the mystery of his will, according to his purpose which he set forth in Christ as a plan for the fullness of time, to unite all things in him, things in heaven and things on earth" (Eph. 1.7-10).

The Church, the Work of Jesus
The Church, then, as a continual work of Jesus Christ through the gift of the Holy Spirit, visibly manifests and symbolizes the action of Christ when we gather to worship the Father with him in the celebration of the eucharist. In this symbolic activity we express, and hence deepen and renew, the presence here of the paschal mystery of Christ, in all its aspects as effective action, sacrificial action, and community-building action. Jesus now is in the state of perfect acceptance by his Father of his perfect act of self-giving. His sacrificial action which reached its highest point in his resurrection from the dead endures eternally, as described in Hebrews 7.23-28. We are told in particular, "Consequently he is able for all time to save those who draw near to God through him, since he always lives to make intercession for them" (Heb. 7.25). The Christian community joins itself in worship with Christ's worship. In the concluding doxology of the Eucharistic Prayer we say: "through Him," for he is our Mediator with the Father, "with Him," for he is our brother like us in all things but sin, and "in Him," for he is our head, the source of our life and worship, "in the unity of the Holy

Spirit," for we are the unity formed by the Holy Spirit, and because of all this, "all glory and honor is yours, Almighty Father, forever and ever. Amen."

This ability of baptized Christians to be united with Christ in his act of worship constitutes the priesthood of all believers. It is referred to by St. Peter when he writes: "But you are a chosen race, a royal priesthood, a holy nation, God's own people, that you may declare the wonderful deeds of him who called you out of darkness into his marvelous light" (1 Pet. 2.9). It is our greatest dignity, our closest association with Christ, our most intimate access to the Father, our deepest sharing in the life of the Spirit. In each one of us its measure is dependent not on ecclesiastical office or human achievement but solely on the reality and intensity of our love, poured into our hearts by the Holy Spirit who is given to us.

DIVERSITY OF GIFTS

The Christian community assembled for worship is not an unstructured gathering of enthusiasts, with each one doing whatever he or she might feel inspired to do. The Body of Christ from the beginning has evidenced a variety of gifts and offices for the upbuilding of the whole. The Gospel according to Luke in the context of the Last Supper has this word about offices among Christians and the way they are to be exercised: "A dispute also arose among them, which of them was to be regarded as the greatest. And he said to them, 'The kings of the Gentiles exercise lordship over them; and those in authority over them are called benefactors. But not so with you; rather let the greatest among you become as the youngest, and the leader as one who serves. For which is the greater, the one who sits at table, or one who serves? Is it not the one who sits at table? But I am among you as one who serves'" (Lk. 22.24-27).

Servants of the Word
We earlier referred to some lists of offices in the Church
given by St. Paul. There have always been in the Christian community "servants of the word" (Lk. 1.2), and
"stewards of the mysteries of God" (1 Cor. 4.1). By
whatever name, some have been called to serve the
Christian community in positions of guidance and lead-
ership: bishops, deacons, apostles, elders, priests,
ministers, etc. These are called on to act in the name of
the community for the welfare of the community. Their
service and activity in connection with the liturgy seems
to be fourfold. 1)Calling the community together as the
assembly of the Christian people. This work of forming
community is not just a matter of posting notices, an-
nouncing times for worship, seeing that the church bell
is rung; it is a continual work of the words and deeds
and whole life of the Christian minister. It is especially
focused in the call to worship. 2) Proclaiming the word,
both in the reading of the Scriptures and in preaching.
3) Leading the prayer of the assembly. 4) Presiding at
the eucharistic celebration; here the leader exercises a
ministerial priesthood, for the sake of, in the service of
the priesthood of the faithful. For the effective symbol of
the paschal mystery of Christ is not just the priest recounting the Last Supper, saying words of consecration
over bread and wine. It is the whole Christian assembly
worshiping God, with the priest presiding in their midst
and expressing the paschal mystery in words.

The priest or minister through ordination or designation
for service within the Church has the function of making
this gathering of individuals be visibly the Christian
people assembled for worship. The ordained minister
also symbolizes the union of this assembly with other
Christian assemblies throughout the world, for ordination is not designation for service of a particular church
merely, but for the whole Church. And finally he sym-

bolizes the continuity of the Christian community in history. This is the meaning of "apostolic succession," understood not merely in a juridical or formalistic way, but organically and vitally, as a visible continuity of life in the Spirit throughout history.

As the priest performs this duty as president of the eucharistic assembly, serving the priesthood of the faithful, he needs to keep a number of elements carefully balanced. It is obviously not sufficient to follow the rubrics exactly. The celebrant must bring his own faith to clear, prayerful expression so as to *lead* the faithful in their worship, in their faith response to the mystery of God's saving grace. While observing substantially the Church's norms for liturgical celebration, careful that all the values and goals intended by those norms are achieved, he must adapt them to the circumstance of time, place, persons, and occasion. Jesus once replied to those who complained that his disciples were not properly observing the prescriptions for the sabbath: "The sabbath was made for man, not man for the sabbath" (Mk. 2.27). Similarly, worship is not for the sake of rubrics, but rubrics for worship. The worship of the Christian Church, while it must be orderly and reverent, should not be the occasion for a new legalism. And, on the other hand, as the priest seeks to make this a genuine community experience for this group of people, he must not lose sight of other dimensions: unity with the Church throughout the world and throughout history, and especially the dimension of worship and adoration: worship of the Father, with Christ, and in the Spirit. For here the words of John are most fully realized: "What we have seen and heard we proclaim also to you, so that you may have fellowship with us; and our fellowship is with the Father and with His Son Jesus Christ" (1 Jn. 1.3).

NOTES

1. See Johannes Behm, *kláo, Theological Dictionary of the New Testament* III, 729-30.

2. *The Phenomenon of Man* (New York: Harper and Row, 1965), p. 294.

Chapter Ten

Prayer without Ceasing

All prayer is bringing to expression our relationship with God, thereby deepening, developing, and strengthening that relationship. There are moments of formal prayer, time we take out to direct our minds and hearts explicitly to God, recalling his present initiative and activity within us and responding to this as sincerely and wholeheartedly as we can. Formal prayer tends especially to increase the *intensive* quality of our relationship with God, through praise, thanksgiving, sorrow, petition, trust, love, and so forth. But our relationship to God, which prayer brings to expression, is not confined to these moments of formal prayer. All the rest of our life as well is rooted in this relationship. Hence formal prayer and our other activities inevitably feed into and influence one another. The ideal of this mutual influence is expressed in a phrase that has biblical roots: "prayer without ceasing." It indicates that the relationship with God which becomes more *intensive* in formal prayer becomes totally *extensive* as well, vivifying and unifying all the encounters, choices, and activities of our lives.

We will consider the matter of prayer without ceasing under three headings: 1) the teaching of Scripture, 2) some reflections and general conclusions drawn from this teaching, and 3) some practical consequences for developing prayer without ceasing.

THE TEACHING OF SCRIPTURE
The Old Testament spirit of prayer without ceasing is reflected in the psalms. "I will bless the LORD at all

161

times; his praise shall continually be in my mouth" (Ps. 34.1), is the opening verse of one psalm. Almost at once the psalmist invites others to join him: "O magnify the LORD with me, let us exalt his name together!" (v. 3). Another psalm tells us: "Trust in him at all times, O people; pour out your heart before him; God is a refuge for us" (Ps. 62.8). This exhortation to continual trust is set in a context that recalls God's protection in the past and hence grounds confidence for the future. The longest of the psalms, Psalm 119, might be called the psalm of continual prayer; it contains many expressions of enduring praise and longing: e.g., "My soul is consumed with longing for thy ordinances at all times" (v. 20). "Seven times a day I praise thee for thy righteous ordinances" (v. 164). "Oh, how I love thy law! It is my meditation all the day" (v. 97). Thus, in the psalms, blessing, praise, trust, and longing for the realization of God's will are given as abiding, continuous aspects of the prayerful person's life.

The language of prayer without ceasing comes especially from the Gospel according to Luke, though here it seems generally to mean insistent, repeated prayer more than a continuous attitude toward God throughout daily life. Thus, Luke 11.5-10 tells the parable of a friend who kept banging on his neighbor's door at midnight, asking for some food to serve an unexpected guest. His persistence is given as a model for effective prayer to God. Later, Luke introduces a similar parable of insistent prayer with the words: "And he [Jesus] told them a parable, to the effect that they ought always to pray and not lose heart" (Lk. 18.1). He then goes on to tell the story of the widow who pestered a judge till he vindicated her, though this judge "neither feared God nor regarded man" (v. 2). Jesus concludes by referring to the elect of God who call to him day and night; they too will be vindicated. A third place in Luke emphasizes the need for continual vigilance and prayer as we await the final coming of the Lord: "But watch at all times, praying that you may have strength to escape all these things that will take place, and to stand before the Son of Man" (Lk. 2 1.36). This final passage does indicate an abiding, prayerful attitude of expectation more than frequent, repeated acts of prayer. Eschatological hope is a motive for prayer without ceasing.

The Letters of Saint Paul
Probably our greatest light on prayer without ceasing in the Bible comes from Paul's letters. The tone is set in the First Letter to the Thessalonians, the earliest of Paul's letters and the first written work of the New Testament. Immediately after the opening greeting, he writes: "We give thanks to God always for you all, constantly mentioning you in our prayers" (v. 2). In this verse he may be referring to often repeated prayer. But toward the end of this letter Paul offers an exhortation to ideal Christian living; in the midst of this he writes: "rejoice always, pray constantly [an earlier translation read: "pray without ceasing"], give thanks in all circumstances; for this is the will of God in Christ Jesus for you" (1 Th. 5. 16- 18). The context of unceasing prayer is here joy and thanksgiving; these are favorite themes in Paul's letters. The whole is summed up under the reflection that this is God's will in Christ Jesus.

The Second Letter to the Thessalonians continues in much the same vein. It opens with a reference to continual thanksgiving: "We are bound to give thanks to God always for you, brethren, as is fitting, because your faith is growing abundantly, and the love of every one of you for one another is increasing" (2 Th. 1.3). A bit further on he speaks of continual prayer for the spiritual welfare of the Thessalonians in a way that is close to the exhortation in Luke 2 1.36 to pray for strength in the eschatological event; after speaking of the second coming, he writes: "To this end we always pray for you, that

163

our God may make you worthy of his call, and may fulfill every good resolve and work of faith by his power" (1.11).

The Letter to the Romans joins together several aspects of the Christian life that should be constant and abiding: zeal, fervor, service of the Lord, joy, patience, and prayer. Paul writes: "Never flag in zeal, be aglow with the Spirit, serve the Lord. Rejoice in your hope, be patient in tribulation, be constant in prayer" (Rom. 12.11-12). He is providing a description of the atmosphere or tone of life of the members of the Body of Christ, of which he was just speaking in verses 3-8.

The three principal Captivity Letters have each some contribution to make for completing Paul's insight into prayer without ceasing. The Letter to the Philippians has an initial reference to repeated prayers of thanksgiving, much as in 1 and 2 Thessalonians (see Phil. 1.3-5). But the final chapter provides another description of the Christian life that joins together many aspects: joy, patience, tranquillity, prayer, thanksgiving, peace. He writes: "Rejoice in the Lord always, again I will say, Rejoice. Let all men know your forbearance. The Lord is at hand. Have no anxiety about anything, but in everything by prayer and supplication with thanksgiving let your requests be made known to God. And the peace of God, which passes all understanding, will keep your hearts and your minds in Christ Jesus" (4.4-7). The Letter to the Colossians at the beginning once again refers to continual thanks for Paul's readers (see 1.3). Later he makes thanksgiving to the Father through Jesus Christ an element of everything we do: "And whatever you do, in word or deed, do everything in the name of the Lord Jesus, giving thanks to God the Father through him" (3.17). The final chapter combines prayer, watchfulness, and thanksgiving as continuous elements in the Christian life: "Continue steadfastly in prayer, being watchful in it with thanksgiving" (4.2). The Letter to the Ephesians points to the foundation of the whole of the Christian life, the Holy Spirit, whose presence is manifested in songs (both inner and outer) and in unceasing thanks for everything: "Be filled with the Spirit, addressing one another in psalms and hymns and spiritual songs, singing and making melody to the Lord with all your heart, always and for everything giving thanks in the name of our Lord Jesus Christ to God the Father" (5.18-20). Toward the end of the letter, he refers again to the Holy Spirit and links his presence to prayer at all times, supplications, and persevering watchfulness: "Pray at all times in the Spirit, with all prayer and supplication. To that end keep alert with all perseverance, making supplication for all the saints" (6.18).

GENERAL CONCLUSIONS FROM SCRIPTURE
The expression "unceasing prayer" has two meanings in Scripture: 1) frequently repeated acts of prayer, returning again and again to praise, thank, and petition God. It is clearly supposed that this kind of unceasing prayer is an integral and normal part of Christian life. And 2) an ongoing quality of life, even outside of times of formal prayer. The express activity of formal prayer overflows to communicate a quality of prayer to the whole of one's life.

Both kinds of unceasing prayer are rooted in the presence of the Holy Spirit. Paul not only tells us to be "aglow with the Spirit" (Rom. 12.11); he also indicates that the Holy Spirit enables us to pray as we ought: "Likewise the Spirit helps us in our weakness; for we do not know how to pray as we ought, but the Spirit himself intercedes for us with sighs too deep for words" (Rom. 8.26). The short letter of Jude gives the same basis for prayer and explains the context surrounding the life of prayer: "Beloved, build yourselves up on your most holy faith; pray in the Holy Spirit; keep yourselves in

165

the love of God; wait for the mercy of Our Lord Jesus Christ unto eternal life" (Jude 20-21). The life of prayer is rooted in the Spirit, for it is he who both establishes us in our relationship to God and enables us to bring this relationship to expression—which is the essential meaning of prayer. For the Spirit makes us adopted children of God the Father, and enables us to cry out "Abba! Father!" (Gal. 4.6); and the Spirit enlightens our hearts with faith in Jesus and enables us to say "Jesus is Lord!" (1 Cor. 12.3).

This relationship to God and its expression in our lives involves, in the view of Scripture, several ongoing, continuous attitudes. We can note at least seven, which seem fairly distinct. The supposition is that these are always present to some degree, though one or another will predominate at a given time:

1) gratitude, thanksgiving for oneself and others;
2) joy, which overflows sometimes in songs, both aloud and in our hearts;
3) peace, living without anxiety, trusting in the Lord the God of peace;
4) patience in difficulties, forbearance in dealing with other people;
5) concern for others, for their needs and hopes as persons loved by God and redeemed by the death of Jesus;
6) watchfulness, an expectancy for the ways God may come into our lives, especially in the eschatological sense;
7) longing for the realization of his will, for the coming of his kingdom.

These ongoing, continuous states of mind and heart flow from periods of formal prayer; they are rooted in the gifts of the Holy Spirit and they express our continuous relationship to God, extending it to all situations, events, and encounters of our lives.

St. John Chrysostom, one of the great commentators on St. Paul from late antiquity,[1] sums up much of what Scripture says about prayer without ceasing in this passage from a homily on prayer:

"Prayer and converse with God is a supreme good: it is partnership and union with God. As the eyes of the body are enlightened when they see light, so our spirit, when it is intent on God, is illumined by his infinite light. I do not mean the prayer of outward observance but prayer from the heart, not confined to fixed times or periods but continuous, throughout the day and night.

"Our spirit should be quick to reach toward God, not only when it is engaged in meditation; at other times also, when it is carrying out its duties, caring for the needy, performing works of charity, giving generously in the service of others, our spirit should long for God and call him to mind, so that these works may be seasoned with the salt of God's love, and so make a palatable offering to the Lord of the universe. Throughout the whole of our lives we may enjoy the benefit that comes from prayer, if we devote a great deal of time to it. . . . Prayer gives joy to the spirit, peace to the heart. I speak of prayer, not words. It is the longing for God, love too deep for words, a gift not given by human agency but by God's grace. The apostle Paul says: 'We do not know how we are to pray but the Spirit himself pleads for us with inexpressible longings.'"[2]

PRACTICAL CONSEQUENCES FOR
PRAYING WITHOUT CEASING
Prayer without ceasing, as a continuous state of soul, is primarily an attitude of heart and will. But it is also a matter of conscious attention to some degree, and of feeling and affectivity as well. Let us say something about each of these.

Love without Ceasing
Our relationship to God, which prayer brings to expression, is grounded in our response to his action and invitation. This response is summed up most fundamentally in keeping the commandment to love God with all our heart and soul and strength and mind (see Lk. 10.27). This love is not a series of single acts, but a continuous attitude and state. It abides at the center of our personalities, as an all-inclusive attitude of our whole selves, deeper than the consciousness of the moment, yet somehow manifested in that consciousness. Our love is sharing in God's love, as John expresses it in 1 John 4.7: "Love is of God, and one who loves is born of God and knows God." This love is poured forth in our hearts by the Holy Spirit, who is given to us (see Rom. 5.5). A person who loves in this way expresses in all he does his relationship to God, that is, he prays.

Abiding Awareness
While continuous prayer consists essentially in this loving attitude of heart and will, it also has a knowing or conscious component as well. A brief reflection will enable us to recognize that our consciousness involves concentric circles of awareness. We have a center of attention that is surrounded by areas of awareness which are more or less intense and gradually reach a fringe where there is scarcely any explicit awareness. I may, for example, be reading a book, and my consciousness is centered on what I am reading. But I am simultaneously aware of other matters: of the chair I'm sitting in, the time of the day, various background noises, a state of weariness, the temperature of the room, reactions of approval or disapproval to what I'm reading, etc. Some of these areas of awareness, these concentric circles of consciousness, are natural and unavoidable at least in some minimal fashion, like being aware of the position of your body, of whether you are alone or with someone, whether you are walking or still. Others are to

some extent acquired, and result from striking experiences in the past, and from strong attitudes of attraction or aversion. A person who has experienced a strong allergic reaction to peanuts will always be aware of whether the food he is eating may contain peanuts or have been prepared with peanut oil, or have some other relationship with peanuts. A person who is strongly attracted to making money will always, in the back of his head, be sizing up every situation for the possibilities it may offer for making a financial profit. A person who finds it very difficult to tolerate loud noises will always be somewhat aware of the noise level in the background. In none of these cases need the matter in question be the center of attention, but it is there as part of the context of conscious awareness.

Our ongoing awareness of God's presence follows this pattern. It is clearly impossible for God to be always the center of attention. But the sovereign love of God which constitutes our profoundest response to his action makes us aware of his presence at the periphery of our attention. We are habitually, at the back of our heads, aware of him in his absolute mystery, as personal, creative; concerned, and saving love. When our minds are released from other matters, they spontaneously turn to him from time to time during the day, and make him at least momentarily the center of attention.

Affective Constancy
Continuous prayer, finally, has an affective or feeling dimension as well. This is not found, of course, in strong affective reactions but in quiet affective states. We have spoken, for example, of joy, thanksgiving, peace, and trust, of patience and forbearance, and of concern and sympathy. Insofar as these are parts of prayer without ceasing, they are not just responses to created values found in situations of human achievement or human suffering. They express also the tran-

scendence of the human spirit, going beyond ourselves and every particular value, to respond to the divine present somehow in the situation. The abiding joy, gratitude, peace, and confidence are rooted in the abiding awareness of God's loving presence, and they serve to sustain and strengthen that awareness. Our ongoing patience and forbearance are a sharing in God's accepting and merciful love for others. Our concern and sympathy reaches out with God's love and embraces others, acknowledging their transcendent dignity as children of God called to everlasting union with him.

Prayer without ceasing is thus first of all an attitude of the will: wholehearted love of God. It is then abiding awareness and quiet affectivity. It finds expression in all that we do, and thus all that we do is prayer. Scripture tells us that we should do all to the glory of God (see 1 Cor. 10.31). This means that our lives should manifest everywhere the divine power and presence at work within us. Jesus tells us the same thing in the Sermon on the Mount when he says, "Let your light so shine before men, that they may see your good works and give glory to your Father who is in heaven" (Mt. 5.16). These are just other ways of speaking of prayer without ceasing.

St. Ignatius Loyola spoke of "finding God in all things." Jerome Nadal, an early companion of Ignatius, described him as "a contemplative even in action." This meant that he found, experienced, and loved God even in the midst of apostolic involvement.

Life with the Living God
It is prayer without ceasing that prevents contemplatives from withdrawing into insensitive isolation from the needs of the world all around them. It likewise prevents socially involved persons from using those whom they appear to serve for their own profit and self-esteem. Prayer without ceasing anchors our lives finally in the totally self-giving love of God for us, and reflects

that love into the world around us. For we open ourselves to receive that gift in receptive love and we extend it to others in active love. This is life lived in the fullness of the Holy Spirit, life with the living God.

NOTES

1. John Chrysostom was born in Antioch in 354. He was ordained deacon in the church of Antioch in 381, and priest in 386. He was a preacher in the cathedral there for twelve years, from 386 until 397, when he was chosen Patriarch of Constantinople. Twice he was sent into exile, because his uncompromising preaching of the gospel made him unacceptable to the imperial court. He died in exile, January 27, 407.

2. Supp., Hom. 6, On Prayer; P.G. 64, 462-466. From the *Liturgy of the Hours,* vol. II, pp. 68-69; English translation by the International Committee on English in the Liturgy, Inc. Some question has been raised about the authenticity of this homily, but its accurate reflection of the Christian understanding of prayer without ceasing is beyond doubt. It is certainly an ancient witness to the meaning and value of this practice.

Recommended Books

Baelz, Peter R. *Prayer and Providence: A Background Study*. New York: Seabury Press, 1968.

Balthasar, Hans Urs von. *Prayer*, A.V. Littledale. New York: Paulist Press, 1967.

Bloom, Anthony. *Beginning to Pray*. New York: Paulist Press, 1971.

Boros, Ladislaus. *Christian Prayer*, trans. David Smith. New York: Seabury Press, 1976.

Boase, Leonard, S.J. *The Prayer of Faith*. Huntington, Ind.: Our Sunday Visitor, 1976.

Breemen, Peter G. van, S.J. *As Bread That is Broken*. Denville, N.J.: Dimension Books, 1974.

Coggan, Donald. *The Prayers of the New Testament*. London: Hodder and Stoughton, 1967.

Daniélou, Cardinal Jean, S.J. *Prayer as a Political Problem*, ed. and trans. J.R. Kirwan. New York: Sheed and Ward, 1967.

Daujat, Jean. *Prayer*, Vol. 37, *Twentieth Century Encyclopedia of Catholicism*, trans. Martin Murphy. New York: Hawthorne Books, 1964.

Doherty, Catherine de Hueck. *Poustinia: Christian Spirituality of the East for Western Man*. Notre Dame, Ind.: Ave Maria Press, 1975.

Farmer, Herbert H. *The World and God, A Study of Prayer, Providence, and Miracle in Christian Experience*. London: Collins, 1963.

Fisher, Fred L. *Prayer in the New Testament*. Philadelphia: Westminister Press, 1964.

Garrigou-Lagrange, Reginald, O.P. *Christian Perfection and Contemplation according to St. Thomas Aquinas and St. John of the Cross*. St. Louis: B. Herder, 1958.

Guillet, Jacques, S.J. *The Religious Experience of Jesus and His Disciples*. St. Meinrad, Ind.: Abbey Press, 1975.

Heiler, Friederich. *Prayer: A Study in the History and Psychology of Religion*, trans. and ed. Samuel McComb and J. Edgar Park. New York: Oxford University Press, 1958.

Heschel, Abraham. *Man's Quest for God: Studies in Prayer and Symbolism*. New York: Charles Scribner's Sons, 1954.

Jeremias, Joachim. *The Prayers of Jesus*, Studies in Biblical Theology, 2nd series, n. 6, trans. John Bowden *et al*. Philadelphia: Fortress Press, 1978.

Loew, Jacques. *Face to Face with God: The Bible's Way to Prayer*, trans. Alan Neame. New York: Paulist Press, 1978.

Merton, Thomas, O.C.S.O. *Contemplative Prayer*. New York: Doubleday, 1971.

Mooney, Christopher, S.J., ed. *Prayer: The Problem of Dialogue with God*. New York: Paulist Press, 1969.

Nedoncelle, Maurice. *God's Encounter with Man: A Contemporary Approach to Prayer*, trans. A. Manson. New York: Sheed and Ward, 1966.

Nouwen, Henri J.M. *Reaching Out: The Three Movements of the Spiritual Life*. New York: Doubleday, 1975.

Simpson, Robert L. *The Interpretation of Prayer in the Early Church*. Philadelphia: Westminister Press, 1965.

Teilhard de Chardin, Pierre, S.J. *The Divine Milieu: An Essay on the Interior Life*. New York: Harper and Row, 1960.

Rahner, Karl, S.J. *On Prayer*. New York: Paulist Press, 1968.

Whelan, Joseph P., S.J. *Benjamin: Essays in Prayer*. New York: Paulist Press, 1974.